D0380228

The Study
of Folk Music in the
Modern World

Officially Withdrawn

Folkloristics
Alan Dundes, General Editor

The Study
of Folk Music in the
Modern World

Philip V. Bohlman

Indiana
University
Press

Bloomington and Indianapolis

"Modal Profile for Europe" is reprinted from Alan Lomax, *Folk Song Style and Culture*, Washington, D.C.: American Association for the Advancement of Science, 1968, by permission of the author. "Mulla Mohammad Jan," is reprinted from Hiromi Lorraine Sakata, *Music in the Mind: The Concept of Music and Musician in Afghanistan*, Kent State University Press, 1983, by permission of the publisher. "*Geming Gequ:* Songs for the Education of the Masses," by Isabel K. F. Wong, is reprinted from Bonnie S. Mc-Dougall, ed., *Popular Chinese Literature and Performing Arts in the People's Republic of China, 1949–1979*, University of California Press, 1984, by permission of the publisher.

© 1988 by Philip V. Bohlman

All rights reserved

No part of this book may be reproduced or utilized in any form or by any means, electronic or mechanical, including photocopying and recording, or by any information storage and retrieval system, without permission in writing from the publisher. The Association of American University Presses' Resolution on Permissions constitutes the only exception to this prohibition.

Manufactured in the United States of America

Library of Congress Cataloging-in-Publication Data

Bohlman, Philip Vilas.
The study of folk music in the modern world.

(Folkloristics)
Bibliography: p.
Includes index.
1. Folk music—History and criticism.   I. Title.
II. Series.
ML3545.B64   1988   781.7'09   87–45401
ISBN 0–253–35555–9
ISBN 0–253–20464–X (pbk.)

1 2 3 4 5 92 91 90 89 88

for
Christine

"All mein Gedanken,
die ich hab',
die sind bei dir."

CONTENTS

FOREWORD

Within folkloristics, there have traditionally been areas of interest which have appealed to an audience outside the academy. Such areas include myth and folk music. More members of the general public are concerned with folk music than with barn-types, or charms, or proverbs, although these genres may also have their devotees.

Certainly it is fair to say that the study of folk music has been crucial for the development of folkloristics. While it may not be possible to establish an absolute starting point for the discipline of folkloristics, two possible candidates for such an honor would surely include Bishop Thomas Percy's (1729–1811) *Reliques of Ancient English Poetry* (1765) and Johann Gottfried Herder's (1744–1803) two-volume *Volkslieder* (1778, 1779), later (1807) entitled *Stimmen der Völker in Liedern*, even though these two pioneers presented the words of folksongs without reference to their music. For this reason, it is essential that any serious scholar of folkloristics be familiar with the concepts and history of folksong within the broader rubric of folk music.

Much of the voluminous writing devoted to the subject of folk music has concentrated upon the traditional musical traditions of rural, illiterate European peasantry. This is in part a reflection and continuation of the excessively narrow definition of "folk" as conceptualized by Herder and those who followed him, e.g., the brothers Grimm. For Herder and the Grimms, the folk was essentially the lower stratum of society, the so-called *vulgus in populo*, the illiterate in a literate society, rural people as opposed to urban people. This overly restrictive definition of folk-as-peasant has unfortunately continued on into the twentieth century. According to this dictum, the music of so-called "primitive" peoples did not qualify as folk music—such peoples were not illiterate (living in a society with a written language) but rather *non*-literate. This is why historically folk music scholars tended to neglect the traditional music of American Indians or black Africans, among others, arguing that such musical heritages should be left for the anthropologist or ethnomusicologist to study. This view is intellectually indefensible insofar as it reflects a nineteenth-century ethnocentric, racist evolutionary bias in which "savages" were presumed to evolve through a stage or stages of barbarism (= peasants) before finally achieving "civilization," the culture of the scholars doing the classifying!

Because of the tenacious persistence of a nineteenth-century classification of the peoples of the world, one finds to this day that folk art refers to European peasant art while "primitive" or "non-Western" art refers to the art of New Guinea, aboriginal Australia, North and South American indigenous populations, etc. The folk/primitive art distinction is an exact parallel for the folk and primitive music dichotomy.

A much more reasonable approach would define various folk groups: ethnic, tribal, national, occupational, religious, familial. All of these folk groups can and do have their own traditional music. Accordingly, one can speak of Greek-American music, Navaho music, Japanese folk music, cowboy folk music, Jewish folk music, and the musical traditions of an individual family. The concept of folk thus becomes much more flexible and applicable worldwide, thereby avoiding the inevitable pitfalls of nineteenth-century evolutionary theorizing.

The Study of Folk Music in the Modern World is one of the very first attempts to consider the subject of folk music from a truly worldwide perspective, free from previous ethnocentric, racist bias. Moreover, its author also succeeds in illuminating the fascinating relationship between folk music and "art music" in various societies.

The author, Philip Bohlman, Assistant Professor in the Department of Music at the University of Chicago, is admirably qualified to have written this important survey of folk music. After earning his B.M. (Piano) in 1975 at the University of Wisconsin, he studied at the University of Illinois with Professor Bruno Nettl, one of the world's authorities on folk music. Bohlman received his doctorate in ethnomusicology in 1984. He has carried out fieldwork in Israel, Germany, and the United States, and he has been an Andrew W. Mellon postdoctoral fellow at the University of Pittsburgh (1984–1985) and a Junior Fellow in the Society of the Humanities at Cornell University (1985–1986). Philip Bohlman's mastery of folk music theory and method is amply demonstrated in this book, which is intended to introduce the subject to a wide audience both within and outside the academy.

Alan Dundes
Berkeley, California

ACKNOWLEDGMENTS

Just as folk music depends on a community to shape it and give it voice, so too does this book owe its existence to several communities of colleagues and friends. While I was a graduate student at the University of Illinois at Urbana-Champaign, it was Bruno Nettl who first taught me to perceive the richness and diversity that folk music reflects in communities close at hand or far away, in communities rooted in their pasts or striving to adapt to a future not yet upon them. During the decade since these first studies in folk music, I have increasingly become aware of my debt to a different sort of teacher, the many musicians and consultants in the communities of the Midwest, western Pennsylvania, West Germany, and Israel where it has been my privilege to engage in fieldwork. The bulk of this book was completed during 1985–86, when I was a Junior Fellow at the Society for the Humanities, Cornell University. I wish to express here my gratitude to Cornell for the generous financial assistance this fellowship provided and to Jonathan Culler, Director of the Society for the Humanities, for assembling a remarkable community of scholars at the Society to guide my thinking and inspire my writing: Anthony Appiah, Bernard Faure, Carlos Fuentes, Barbara Harlow, Victor Koschmann, Uday Mehta, Giovanni Pettinato, F. Jamil Ragep, Wole Soyinka, Gayatri Chakravorty Spivak, and Alan Wolfe. My tenure at Cornell was all the richer because it afforded me the opportunity to profit from the abundant counsel and wisdom of William W. Austin. Alan Dundes invited me to contribute this book to the series Folkloristics at Indiana University Press, and I am grateful to him for his trust in me. I should also like to thank him for the many intensive hours that the two of us spent plumbing the marvelous holdings in folk music at the University of California at Berkeley, where I held a visiting faculty position in the fall of 1984. This book has benefited in ways too numerous to list here from the careful readings of its earlier incarnations by Katherine Bergeron, Alan Dundes, and Bruno Nettl; I thank them for their willingness to suggest ways of improving the manuscript, and I apologize if my intransigence has caused me to fall short of the standards they would have me meet. Much encouragement and assistance from Indiana University Press guided this book along its transformation of the oral to the written. During recent years I have experienced the formation, however incipient, of a new community of folk music: my family. Listening to my children, Andrea and Benjamin, has taught me much about oral tradition, the origins of folk music, and the ability of folk music to express the most profound of human values. As in all communities of folk music, this one has its primary musician, my wife, Christine Wilkie Bohlman. I am confident that there could be few better records of my gratitude to Christine than the old German folk song that accompanies the dedication of this book to her.

Philip V. Bohlman
Chicago, Illinois

INTRODUCTION

> This is what a folk song realy is the folks
> composes there own songs about there own
> lifes an there homefolks that live around
> them.
>
> Aunt Molly Jackson (Greenway 1953:8)

In 1981, the International Folk Music Council (IFMC) adopted a new name, the International Council for Traditional Music (ICTM). Professional societies do such things, of course, usually to signal that they are about to redefine their fields of study with greater precision. We can surely imagine that, by 1981, the IFMC might have honed its theoretical acumen sufficiently during its almost thirty-five years of existence to suggest the need for reconsideration of its name and the object of its study. But *traditional music* hardly seems more precise than *folk music*. Yes, folk music forms traditions, but so do other genres of music. One can speak about traditions of Italian opera or traditions of South Indian classical music without provoking battles over the use and abuse of terminology. No one could deny that the diverse musics and musical cultures studied by the members of the IFMC constituted many types of tradition; accordingly, to dub them traditional music in the concerted voice lent by a scholarly journal, international meetings, and myriad national committees was not to force musical repertories into molds that few thought would fit. Indeed, the change was not so much a result of believing in traditional music as of losing faith in folk music.

The symbolic repudiation of folk music by the ICTM was hardly an isolated instance of a momentary fall from grace. By the 1980s, folk music had fallen on hard times in the academic world. It still succored a coterie of ardent believers, and it continued to designate panels at scholarly meetings or courses in college catalogues. Closer scrutiny of this folk music study, however, would reveal an increasingly conservative undertow. Several sacred repertories—the Child ballads, for example—always managed to spawn their share of publications, whether to proclaim yet another system for modal classification or to announce yet another version of "Edward" in a community where Anglo-American influences were previously undocumented. Ironically, it was this conservative voice that insisted most vigorously on the need for precision, or at least an imagined precision, that could guard true folk music from the sullying inflections of other genres or the mass media. Precision thus meant concentrating on the precious while situating folk music in the past.

The conservative voice of folk music scholarship, however, exemplified only one approach to the panoply of musics that musicologists of Western art music did not include in their purview. Popular music, non-Western music, country music—all of these and their complex components were attracting increasing interest from different disciplines; if the generic categories were somewhat blurred and constantly undergoing change, there was a consensus that interdisciplinary approaches were the most valuable way of understanding the new subgenres of folk music. A few scholars began recognizing folk music in new contexts: bluegrass, urban revivals, mass-mediated traditions. There was no particular insistence that these contexts *were* folk music, only that folk music was a part of them. Thus, an alternative voice for folk music scholarship emerged. Rather than expressing concern over the disappearance of folk music, it preferred to see change as normative and creative; rather than subscribing to restrictive categories that limited folk music to rural venues, it ascribed importance to place on the basis of community, the aggregate of individuals that interacts with its physical and cultural environment. The concerns of this alternative voice, however, drifted farther and farther away from its conservative counterpart, and it seemed that the voices had very different visions of what folk music really was.

Since its inception in 1947, the International Folk Music Council had provided a forum for conflicting views of folk music. In the editorial that inaugurated the first issue of the IFMC's journal in 1949, conservative and progressive issues both appear, if, in fact, the conservative are not a bit more pressing. Whereas there is recognition that the "fashions and amusements of the city are all-pervasive," urgency is not to be underestimated because "we have to face the fact that folk music is disappearing as a traditional art" (Editorial 1949:1). The founders of the IFMC were not remiss when it came to facing-the-fact and therefore took as their first objective—stated in their constitution and reiterated for years inside the title page of their journal—"to assist in the preservation, dissemination and practice of folk music of all countries" (The International Folk Music Council: Its Formation and Progress 1949:4). This was an activist agenda, aimed at stemming disappearance by changing those conditions disadvantageous to folk music's survival. If that meant staging revivals, so be it; if it meant actively soliciting government agencies and the mass media, that too must be. One cannot ignore an overt consciousness of the past in this agenda, but equally overt is the injunction that folk music must not be relegated to the past. Staking out a place for folk music in the modern world quickly became a raison d'être for the IFMC.

If folk music was to be delivered from its projected demise, the IFMC was certainly a likely candidate for rescuer. It had cast its theoretical nets as widely as possible while still identifying folk music as the explicit object of its study. The broad international base of the IFMC encouraged many perspectives and produced a literature that discussed folk music throughout the world, thereby maintaining a theoretical framework that stressed comparison. Throughout its early years the pronouncements of the IFMC, though often forged through fiery debate, nonetheless reflected considerable latitude and willingness to make concessions on what was or was not to fit under the folk music aegis. Even the most conservative stalwarts of the IFMC, such as Maud Karpeles, long one of the council's most powerful voices, wrote periodically in a vein that could sound positively liberal.

Eventually, however, the position of folk music was not secure. Those who engaged in the internecine squabbles that effected its ouster from the official name of the professional society seemed unable to agree on what was wrong with the term, only that something was not quite right. One position held that *folk music* was too specific; another that it was too general. One side contended that tradition rather than folk constituted the real focus; another countered that tradition was nothing if not animated by the folk. In the end, little ballyhoo accompanied the actual transformation from one name to the other. No editorial in the yearbook of the council mentions the change, justifies it, or even issues an apologia; outsiders note the change only because of the yearbook's new title. Few members have objected strenuously in subsequent years, and the ambiguous nature of traditional music seems not the least bit contentious. One might think that folk music has quietly slipped into the past and peacefully become a relic of a less complicated age. One might imagine that folk music has confronted and been confronted by the modern world, but that the resulting impasse meted out no terrain appropriate for survival. This book argues otherwise and proposes an alternative interpretation of folk music in the modern world.

Recent years have witnessed considerable criticism of the most fundamental concepts of folk music. In its most extreme form, this criticism has questioned the basic validity of recognizing any genre of music and folklore that could rightfully be called folk music. Less vehement but equally ideological in thrust, another form of criticism has taken a strictly historicist stance, recognizing the existence of folk music but only under conditions that obtained in a simpler era, which by definition would not be possible today. Much of this criticism asserts that folk music as a concept of aesthetic and cultural expression has outlived its usefulness. Like the ICTM, critics seem less concerned that the realm of study is wrong than that those who undertake it as a livelihood are wrongheaded. Hence, one observes a certain thrashing about in search of surrogate names. Most consistent and specific among the suggestions is "working-class" music or the like (Harker 1985 and Keil 1982; cf. also Greenway 1953). As attractive as the working-class-cum-folk seems at first glance, its advocates always advance their claims tentatively—that is to say, unconvincingly—and not uncommonly with an appendix of other surrogate terms (Keil 1978:264). The most important point that this criticism should drive home, however, is that the concept "folk music" is in need of considerable overhaul and that we need to wrench its moorings from a cultural setting that no longer exists, if it ever did.

The cultural setting with which I am primarily concerned in this book is the modern world. This setting is responsive to both dramatic change and the stability afforded by tradition. It is a setting in which folk music thrives, albeit with only occasional resemblance to the pristine models advocated by conservative scholarship. This book is therefore less an account of folk music itself than an appraisal of the study of folk music. It takes as a fundamental premise that folk music surrounds us in abundance and that the study of folk music helps us understand the diverse panoply of aesthetic and cultural meanings that such abundance bespeaks. The study of folk music must address such musical abundance in all its diversity or become increasingly parochial and moribund, a field devoted wistfully to a rosy past that might have been.

That this book takes a stance of broadening the field is obvious from the title, which states the subject of the field as folk music, not folk song. This distinction is far more than simply adding a dash of instrumental music to the disciplinary broth. It multiplies the ways one can define a folk music community; it allows for new processes of change; it acknowledges many canons rather than one whose hypothetical centrality is prescribed by language; it draws the core and boundaries of a musical culture closer together and admits that their interaction is very complex. The ramifications of stating the field as "the study of folk music" are many. Not only does one encounter more music, but more theories come to bear upon that music; not only does one broaden the social basis of music, but it becomes readily apparent that comparable social bases exist throughout the world. Redesignating the object of the field as folk music ipso facto poses new questions about change and modernism, about the different ways music functions in non-Western cultures.

The study of folk music necessarily entails more than much of the literature devoted to folk song would indicate. Folk music from this disciplinary perspective is not limited to Europe or North America; nor need it be rural and particularly old; nor does it circulate solely through oral transmission. These are the restrictive caveats of an earlier scholarship that the study of folk music intentionally supersedes. In so doing, it is able to muster new perspectives from other fields, with whose goals and methods the study of folk music intersects. The anthropological and sociological examination of community, the folkloristic study of expressive behavior, the ethnomusicological concern for music throughout the world—these theoretical thrusts and more contribute to the study of folk music for which this book argues. Thus, whatever the new issues and directions this book might advance, it is not advocating a start from scratch. Its call, rather, is for a reassessment of *how* we think about the folk music we encounter in the world, which in turn will free us from thinking only about *what* folk music is. Accordingly, as this book forges a more inclusive understanding of folk music's diversity in the modern world, the study of folk music will broaden its position considerably among the humanistic and social sciences.

Given the somewhat revisionist tone that I have set forth, what theoretical perspectives remain open to us? Two general perspectives suggest themselves. First, sufficient collections and research facilities exist to enable us to do purely historical and descriptive studies of musical cultures that contained musical activity approximating many of the criteria accepted as folk music. This approach is conservative and safe, and it still has much to offer to folk music scholarship. Second, folk music research might begin assuming a more inductive approach, based on observations of musical activity that continues to display many aspects of folk music, even against the backdrop of a modernized and urbanized world. Not so safe as the first approach, this one requires forays far beyond the borders of the traditional definitions of folk music. It will soon be evident that, for the most part, this book takes the second approach. In doing so, the book argues not for a complete redress of conservative approaches but for a substantial addition to them. Thus, it posits that the subgenres of folk music today are quite different from those described when folk music scholarship first began to develop in the nineteenth century. Again, I do not necessarily claim that the older subgenres no longer exist—many of them do—but that relentless preoccupation with them has blinded many scholars to the emergence of new subgenres developing from the old and benefiting from the changing social bases of folk music.

This book incorporates two large cultural contexts for folk music that have previously been tangential, if not anathema, to much folk music scholarship: non-Western cultures and modern society. The extension to non-Western settings has always been part of a claim to universality that many have wished on folk music. My reasoning here is somewhat different, for I am less concerned with universality than with particularity, that is, locating folk music in social structures that are unlike those in Europe and North America. I believe it essential also to understand how folk music appears in the modern world if we are to avoid demoting it to the status of an archaic genre. That this unequivocal association of folk music with urban environments and technological means of dissemination will challenge long-held notions about what folk music should be is an inevitable and fitting outcome of this approach.

Defining *folk music* has always been a tempting and dangerous undertaking for the scholars of the field (cf. Elbourne 1975). The IFMC wrangled over definitions for years, admitting, on one hand, the impossibility of an all-purpose definition but arguing, on the other, that "provisional declarations" must stipulate certain elements (General Report 1953:12). In this study I avoid offering a single definition of *folk music*. There are two reasons for this, which I hope will prevent some detractors from accusing me of simply bowing out of a responsibility. First, the different contexts of folk music that I investigate here yield very different definitions. To apply many of the most common definitions of *folk music* in European and North American society to the Middle East would be a pointless and thankless undertaking. Second, because I regard change as ineluctably bound to folk music tradition, I also assert that the dynamic nature of folk music belies the stasis of definition. Thus, whereas it is safe to say that many of the characteristic definitions of *folk music* were once widely applicable to rural society, they are less so today; quite the contrary, it becomes increasingly evident that folk music is not eschewed by the city, thereby requiring any attempt at definition to take the urban context into consideration.

Rather than employing strict definitions, this study addresses the components of folk music by seeking to understand the interaction in dual or binary structures. I choose binary structures and most often couch them as dialectics for several reasons fundamental to the approaches urged by this book. Dialectic has an essentially dynamic quality, and I mean it here to serve as a metaphor for ongoing and continuous change. Thus, change ensues from the contraposition in dialectics of such elements as text and context, product and process, oral tradition and written tradition, synchrony and diachrony, and cultural core and boundary. The consistency with which I employ dialectical reasoning is intended as a leitmotif, lending a certain unity and comparability to the overall theoretical approach. Different dialectical approaches render this unity multidimensional, showing it to be a metaphor for yet another concern central to this study, modernism. If dialectical concepts sometimes act as ersatz definitions, they nevertheless draw attention to the more specific components of folk music. I address the question of community, for example, as a dialectic between cultural core and boundary; the boundary through its contact with the outside admits change to the folk music tradition of a community, while the core undergirds the centrality of certain cultural activities and musical repertories. Canon, though often construed as static, is here considered to be dynamic because of its dialectical bridging of text and context.

Folk music scholarship inherited its conservative tone from the earliest stages of its history, at least from the mid–eighteenth century and Johann Gottfried Herder's vision of a folk whose aesthetic creativity sprang from nature. Exceptional has been the perspective that did not turn toward the past, idealizing and revering a community of folk music that was just out of reach and then fretting over the best ways to rescue folk music before it disappeared. Many of the fundamental endeavors of folk music scholarship are steeped in this conservatism and the ideological stances it engenders: collection, classification, revival, canonization. Even seemingly liberal and radical ideologies frequently turn up a conservative side when applied to folk music; for example, transforming folk music into working-class music requires a faith in the ability of the working class to cohere as a community not unlike the faith that imagines a coherent folk community.

There can be no question that folk music scholarship rarely lacks ideological leanings; if these often sanction its conservative portrayal of the past, they also quicken a tendency toward particularity and diverse viewpoints. For this book to claim a perspective purified of ideology would therefore fail to address folk music on the preferred turf of its chief scholars. This I would not pretend to do. But I do not undertake this text as an ideological position in itself; rather, I attempt to design for it a range of alternative ideological strategies that touch on as many issues central to the study of folk music as possible. Instead of looking at the past and idealizing it, instead of fussing about saving folk music before it discharges its last gasp, I call for the study of folk music in the modern world and in the incredibly diverse contexts that folk music now freely admits. I challenge conservative ideologies from several angles in relation to both the objects on which such ideologies focus and the ways in which they formulate theory. For example, I persistently call attention to the importance of the individual folk musician as an agent of change and creativity. Similarly, I insist on the need to accept external influences and their inseparability from internal change. Thus, folk musicians may be exceptional individuals more often than homogenized versions of everyman. And I place great importance on investigating folk music in new settings—cities, the mass media, popular genres— and on accepting folk music as the product of new cultural processes, especially modernization and urbanization.

It would be unmitigated delusion to deny that conservative ideological stances have generated a pall of doom that has afflicted much folk music scholarship in the past and continues to suppress the development of new approaches. It is perhaps comforting to some that a conservative ideology prods them to yearn for the past and a simpler life. In contrast, it will make the more skeptical wonder whether there really no longer is a genre appropriately called folk music and whether, after all, it might be better just to capitulate to a more neutral terminology, say, traditional music. But folk music, by the very nature of its capacity for change, asks us to consider alternative strategies as well. Rather than contenting ourselves with an ideology of conservatism, why not look instead at the proliferation of changing contexts for creativity in the modern world? And why not reformulate our canons of folk music in recognition of the new texts that change has yielded to folk music?

*The Study
of Folk Music in the
Modern World*

ONE

The Origins of Folk Music, Past and Present

The elements of music are in every thing
around us; they are found in the chirpings of
the feathered choristers of nature; in the
voices or calls of various animals; in the mel-
ancholy sound of the waterfall, or the wild
roar of the waves; in the hum of distant mul-
titudes, or the concussion of sonorous bodies;
in the winds, alike when their dying cadence
falls lightly on the ear as it gently agitates the
trees of the forest, as when the hurricane
sweeps around, and in terrific accents betrays
the voice of Him, who "Rides in the whirl-
wind, and directs the storm."

William C. Stafford (1830:1–2)

The question of origin cannot be solved.
The beginnings of music are lost in the days
of yore, as are the rudiments of speech, religion, and the dance. All we can achieve is to
follow these manifestations back to the time
when the curtain slowly rose over the earliest
act of mankind's history.

Curt Sachs (1962:39)

In the Beginning . . .

Logic would seem to dictate placing a chapter on origins at the beginning of
this book. Caution, however, suggests otherwise. Formerly a subject for considerable debate and theoretical machination of fantastic proportions, the search
for origins has more recently subsided quietly, earning only a few footnotes
that relegate it to a more innocent age of folk music scholarship. The apologia

for this retreat is simple: "We can't really know anything definite about origins." It is not easy to offer a rejoinder to such a caveat because one confronts the need to make some rather hefty claims for new discoveries or previously unknown evidence. Or does one? Discoveries, evidence: that is the stuff of a primordial past, of *the* origins. Yes, many of our scholarly forebears were in search of just such origins. But theirs was a restricted view of origins, predicated by a primary concern for data, facts, and material products: the first scale, the first form of bone flute or slit drum, the link between speech and song. There is also a broader context for origins, one that concerns itself not so much with products but with the processes of coming into being. How does a society create new songs? Whence arises musical change? When and how do new canons of folk music form? These questions, too, require speculation and often yield only tentative answers. I hesitate to claim that they are more germane to the study of folk music than were earlier explorations for ancient origins. If they are more fashionable, they too leave one wondering at times whether it is really possible to "know anything definite about origins." Caution makes its case even stronger.

If theoretical concern for the origins of folk music has, at least on the surface, waned, the legacy of theories accounting for origins lingers and continues to underlie many contemporary conceptions and misconceptions about folk music. I choose not to bow to caution's warnings, then, not because I would posit a new theory but because I prefer to counter with an observation that necessitates abandonment of more circumspect approaches: the need to relate folk music to its beginnings persists as an essential and pervasive component of folk music theory. Aesthetic and textual concerns, for example, often presume an understanding of origins. An authentic version of a folk song is one that has demonstrable links to an *Urtext*, however abstractly or factitiously it has been formulated. Oral tradition, however dynamically it is portrayed, reflects various theories pro and contra different types of origin. The narrative of an epic in oral tradition may speak to real events in the life of a historical figure, or it may be an allegory more generally representative of the human condition. Accordingly, the origins are local or universal or some combination thereof. The social constructs of folk music, too, originate in different ways, as do different repertories and styles of performance practice. The persistent pursuit of origins belies the inability to "know anything definite."

The search for the sources of folk music has produced anything but unequivocal results. One can safely say that there are as many concepts of the origins of folk music as there are theories of folk music; few of the field's basic issues remain untouched. A survey of these concepts, therefore, is a historiographic approximation of the entire field. Logic, so it seems, was not wrong to suggest starting in this way. The effect of surveying concepts of origin has the further result of revealing a vast range of musical activities acknowledged as folk music, and that, of course, fits well with my intent to cast off many of the restrictive shackles clamped on folk music. Concomitantly, this survey aims to illustrate the need to expand the theoretical tolerance for folk music in the modern world. To effect such an expansion, I shall urge two basic temporal frameworks for the discussion of origins: a relatively remote past, about which we indeed can only theorize; and the more recent past, especially as it is in the process of becoming the present. A rejuvenated quarrel of Ancients and Moderns? Not quite, for I do not pit past and present against each other. Instead, I would superimpose the present and the past, suggesting that basic claims for nebulous and idealized origins continue. All too often, this persistence further entrenches beliefs that folk music should play an archetypal social role and embody an unrealizable aesthetic purity. It does not play such a role and never did. The folk music of the past was not substantially different—functionally or aesthetically—from the folk music of today. Folk songs no more composed themselves in a bygone golden age than in a modern, industrialized world. The origins of folk music in the present are just like those of the past.

Of Gods, Birds, and the Music of the Spheres

The panoply of origin theories reflects a remarkable range of concepts about folk music. Some of these concepts stress musical elements; others stress cultural roots. Some shroud folk music in numinous mists; others specify every milestone along the path of development. Most attempts to locate the sources of music do not take on the whole of creation. There have been theories, of course, that have extended speculation about the parts to the whole, thereby attracting the cynicism and criticism of a later generation. This relative specificity may well result from the use of the past to explain the present, even the idealized present; scholars concentrated on finding explanations for those aspects that concerned them the most. At the end of the nineteenth century, for example, the evolution from simple to complex forms was of paramount importance to folk music scholars, inspiring them to generate a multitude of models that would explain music's many positions on an evolutionary ladder. The more reactionary mode of scholarship, insisting that folk music could only endure in rural settings, quite appropriately divined ways of situating folk music's origins in venues completely untouched by urbanization or modernization. One might say, therefore, that the origins of folk music often proved a point; they explained folk music as it was, or as it ought to be.

The origin of music per se. The broadest conceptualization of origins attempts to explain the very existence of music. Myth, for example, often contains a variety of explanations of music, often as a salient component of creation itself.

Occasionally, music is the invention of an individual god, such as Apollo, or of a figure presumed to be mortal and real, such as the biblical Yuval. Myth, which uses natural phenomena to explain the material world of society, offers similar explanations for music. Myth may regard music as a link to a supernatural world or mimesis of the sounds of this world. Music may come into being in very specific ways, exhibiting a high degree of differentiation, or as a general, undefined realm of sounds.

Mythological explanations of the origins of music may be on the whole more general, but they are not the only explanations that cast their theoretical nets around all musical phenomena. Psychological approaches, like those guiding early comparativists Richard Wallaschek and Carl Stumpf, plumbed the beginnings of music to ascertain the motivation of music-making (Wallaschek 1893 and Stumpf 1911). A concern for the human impulse to music-making has also consistently guided the work of John Blacking, who focuses this concern on psychophysiological questions (cf. 1973 and elsewhere). Psychological and biological investigations accept a sort of universality related to evolution—that it is fundamental to the human species to express oneself with music. "All members of the species are basically as capable of dancing, singing and making music, as they are of speaking a natural language. There is even evidence that early human species were able to dance and sing several thousand years before *homo sapiens sapiens* emerged with the capacity for speech as we now know it" (Blacking 1981:9). In essence, music's origins were coeval with the beginning of culture.

The origin of social and musical functions. Somewhat more specific than the origins of music per se is the equation of express social functions with the development of music. Music therefore articulates the organization of society. It may do so by dint of its role in ritual or by transforming labor into a communal, rather than individual, activity. The early Romantics even went so far as to assert that folk music provided an infrastructure to a stratum, the *Mutterschicht* (mother level), that had achieved an idealized social harmony (Danckert 1966:22–27).

Particularity characterizes in still other ways the search for origins in musical functions. Generative theories of musical grammar, for example, posit the preexistence (or inevitability) of certain patterns and structures (e.g., Lerdahl and Jackendoff 1983). One of the most persistent paths to particularity has resulted in the distinction between theories that anchor music in either speech or movement. The speech theories concentrate more on song, the movement theories more on dance and instrumental music. A lasting result of these approaches to origin has been the somewhat disparate directions pursued by scholars studying folk song and those describing their field as folk music.

The origin of musical style. Musical style is an aspect of the sharing of repertories by groups of individuals formed on the basis of social cohesion. The origin of musical style, therefore, is removed completely from the indistinguishable past. In some theories the point of removal from the ancient past—from what was once called "primitive music"—is specified; Hubert Parry (and several notable successors, including Cecil Sharp) believed that this point occurred when two phrases took the place of a single, formless melodic line (Parry 1910:47–61 and Sharp 1965:42–43). Just as style changes, so too do musical repertories admit the possibility of new origins, which may be either internal or external to the group. Depending on the style and structure of repertory, the innovation permitted by renewed origins may occur frequently or extend over long periods. A particular style of oral-formulaic epic composition may stabilize the tradition for centuries; small, volatile political groups may assemble an ad hoc style from a pastiche of preexistent repertories. Stylistic origins often constitute a specific chronology and historical development.

The origin of a piece. The identification of certain discrete entities such as pieces exists in almost all folk music traditions. Most traditions, moreover, distinguish several ways of determining how pieces originate. These ways may be specific—recognition of a composer or the narrative description of a real event—or general, like the dream sources of most songs among the North American Flathead (Merriam 1967:3–24). Internal and external systems of classification often depend on the ways in which new pieces originate. Advocates of monogenesis or polygenesis—the single or multiple birth of similar pieces—often disagree sharply on how to define the relation between one piece and others that sound very much like it (cf. List 1978). Some of the most common forms of aesthetic judgment also require a concept of origins. Claiming that true folk music is ageless requires the presumption of great but indefinite periods of time between the inception of tradition and the contemporary performance of it. Judgments of this sort may even place quite strict limits on what is and is not admissible to the folk music canon.

The elements smaller than the piece. In practice this category often overlaps with the preceding ones; in principle it serves as the antipode to accounts of theories concerned primarily with the origins of music in general. Musical change often rests on the ability of a tradition to tolerate new elements entering individual pieces. Change in many European traditions originates at the sub-piece level, often appearing first in variant performances. Elements of stylistic change, too, often enter the tradition in the form of small motifs or the alteration of a single phrase. As one tradition comes in contact with others, individual elements lend themselves to acculturation, thereafter functioning as new points of origin for certain aspects. This may occur in relatively random fashion, or it may parallel the broader social and historical changes through which a culture passes. In the case of Shawnee musical style, for example, Bruno Nettl has distinguished four historical moments that admitted new possibilities of stylistic genesis, each moment related directly to migration or relocation of Shawnee communities (1956:138–39).

As these theories concentrate on increasingly limited concepts and structures, they become more concerned with origins in the recent past or present. Discussion of the origin of music itself resorts to consideration of the prehistoric past, whether couched in the language of myth or the empirical constructs of natural science. Theories that attempt to cover all music rarely break down their evidence to explain the origin of individual pieces, which anyway can scarcely be discerned in a primordial era. Speculation about how individual elements enter a tradition hardly affords the opportunity to extrapolate from a time for which there is no knowledge of the specific contemporary traditions. Common to these diverse approaches, however, is the desire to explain musical tradition by understanding how its historical antecedents came about. Again we see that the search for origins reflects the urge to know both the past and the present.

Origins: From Metaphysical to Human Determination

Whether mythological or biological, ageless or explicitly functional, the origins of folk music exhibit two causational extremes, with a third position characterizing various compromises between these extremes. At one extreme, causation assumes multifarious ontological forms, most often without any historical specificity. At the other, folk music originates because of the acts of a single creator or composer, for whom there is at least speculation regarding identity and historical position. Compromises between these extremes often interpret the causation of folk music as a process of constantly coming into being; history, cultural factors, and personality are assumed to be of importance, but they are sometimes accorded an almost agnostic anonymity or irrelevance. All three of these positions survive in contemporary folk music theory.

Metaphysical origins of folk music. Theories of folk music that regard it as coming into existence by itself often stress communality and collectivity, even when these forces are occasionally disguised as natural phenomena. The *Volksgeist*, or folk spirit, was explicable only insofar as it was an expression of nature and retained intangible roots in nature. The earliest theories to concern themselves with folk music itself—those of Johann Gottfried Herder and Jacob Grimm, for example—fused nature and folk society. When Herder did specify the characteristics of "the folk," he preferred to see them as "wild" and "lacking social organization" *(unpolizirt)*, that is, closer to nature so that they could be more responsive to "nature's poesy" *(Naturpoesie)* (Herder 1779 and Danckert 1966:5–8). Denying that a folk song could have a composer, Grimm announced that "a folk song composes and transmits itself" (Danckert ibid.:9).

We may wonder if these formulations were not fanciful even at the beginning of the nineteenth century, but we should not ignore the aspects of innovation that made them attractive to subsequent generations. Folk music was essentially secular, the product of natural rather than divine inspiration. Nature came to play a central role in the shaping of folk music theory, just as it was important in other aesthetic formulations from the mid–eighteenth century to the present (cf. Kivy 1984, esp. 7–9; see also Sebeok 1979:39–40). The manifestation of nature in folk music, however, became gradually less mimetic, achieving instead the status of immanence: folk music, if not a reflection of nature, is at least "natural." Accordingly, theorists came to observe the laws of natural science in folk music, which conveniently provided the opportunity to employ evolutionary interpretations. So profound was the influence of Darwinian theory on folk music scholars that it was not unusual when Cecil Sharp stated baldly that "the life history of a folk song . . . is clearly a case of evolution" (1965:21).

How nature succored folk music was a more controversial question. Two general theories have been at odds from Herder's day until the present: origins in speech versus origins in movement. Disputants have at times bitterly contested these two theories, which persist in such bifurcation as the one between theory that concerns itself largely with the texts of folk song and theory whose focus is the contextual functions of instrumental folk music. It is not surprising that the argument in favor of speech as origin had the earliest supporters. Herder was a literary historian; the Grimms were linguists; Arnim and Brentano, the compilers of *Des Knaben Wunderhorn* (1806/1808), were poets. Folk music was a vehicle for words, for poetry.

The speech theory has four main variants. First, folk music was an artistic form that united speech and music. Second, speech and music had their origins in similar expressive functions, whether in forms of protospeech and protomusic (cf. Nettl 1956:136) or in genres of folklore such as the *cante-fable* (Wiora 1965:40). Third, speech gradually became music after passing through the intermediate stage of "impassioned speech" (Nettl 1956:135). The final variant has resulted from a somewhat unrelated linguistic formulation, one proffered by semiotics, which asserts that speech and music (and movement, for that matter) communicate abstractly as signs and that they may enhance their functions as agents of communication when combined (Sebeok 1979:39–40 and Hanna 1979:221–23).

The search for music's origins in movement owed a great debt to evolutionary theory. Movement theories often turned to evolution for data and models of explanation, benefiting greatly from the growth of comparative approaches to natural science in the late nineteenth century. The earliest movement theories drew more directly from Herbert Spencer than from Darwin (e.g., Wallaschek 1893:235). The essence of almost all movement theories is the equation of movement with rhythm. Several types of aesthetic activity arise directly from rhythm, the most obvious being music and dance and their interrelation (Keal-iinohomoku 1972:387). Rendered in more social scientific terms, movement organizes social functions, involving groups of people in individual activities. The movement theories plotted specific paths for the evolution of music (see Sachs 1962). Rhythm yielded melodic intervals; intervals strung together became melodies; contrast in melodic fragments established rudimentary form (Wallaschek 1893:233). Musical instruments, too, developed as means of articulating rhythm, thereby reinforcing movement's essentially musical impetus (Sachs 1940:25–26). Whereas speech theories stressed music's communicative potential in society, movement theories often concentrated on social function, the role of movement in the aesthetic organization of ritual, play, and social coherence. Not surprisingly, the scholars most concerned with the origin of music in movement were anthropologists and other social scientists, and vehement debates arose between them and the scholars who turned to speech in search of musical origins.

Composition as genesis. At a superficial level the notion of creator is not absent from some of the earliest theories claiming a natural origin for folk music. Mythological origins, for example, might well claim a supernatural creator, specifying the way in which music or a specific instrument appeared among mortals. More empirically, individuals became associated with the creation of folk music, in part because they were observed in the act of composition but also as a radical redress of those theories that were reconnoitering the gray fogs of primordial eras for origins. Such beliefs were simply held to be untenable and impractical in their explanations of contemporary change. It is arguable that even the earliest folk music theorists did not completely eschew the contribution of individuals (Wiora 1971a). Attacks against the idealized concepts of the nineteenth century were often polemical on exactly the question of composition. Most notable among the polemicists was Phillips Barry (1961), who insisted that individual musicians created individual songs. Barry won followers in Cecil Sharp and Ralph Vaughan Williams, who, like Barry, regarded communal influence as a process of creating variations; what Barry called "communal re-creation" Sharp termed "communal authorship" (Sharp 1965:12–13 and Vaughan Williams 1954:55–58; cf. Karpeles 1951:11–12). Ernst Klusen has been especially vehement in his attempts to redress the idealization of folk music by earlier German scholars, and he calls for replacement of the term

Volkslied with *Gruppenlied* (group song), hoping thereby to achieve a more realistic assessment of the process of folk music creation and transmission (Klusen 1969, 1973, and 1986).

The theories perceiving the origins of folk music in the acts of individuals permit considerable latitude in the ways composition takes place. The composer may use either oral or written techniques. A composed piece may use relatively new melodic material, or it may borrow from previously existing pieces. Contrafaction, the application of an existing melody to a new text, is commonplace for certain subgenres. Composition seldom fixes a single version, even when the composer inscribes the piece first in a written format.

In contrast, very different theories account for questions of compositional motivation and social venue. Some theorists call for universality, claiming that humans naturally create (Blacking 1973 and Sharp 1965:42). Others prefer to cast creativity in the context of specialization. The circulation of folk songs on single sheets of paper—broadsides or broadsheets—may involve considerable specialization. Not only is there a specific composer, but a new song may require engravers, printers, illustrators, street hawkers, and even street performers. Each of them, however, plays a creative role in establishing the link between written and oral tradition. The involvement of individual specialists in folk music traditions also raises ideological issues concerning the transformation from composed piece to community property and the remuneration or exchange of goods that marks innovation within the tradition. Implicit in any close consideration of the composer's role is the rebuttal of locating the origins of folk music in the *Volksgeist* or the idealized egalitarian society of a golden past.

Folk music in a process of coming into being. The compromises between metaphysical origins and individual determination range widely. Most of them accept, nevertheless, that folk music tradition admits new pieces that are the products of individuals but then submits them to a scrutiny that originates in the community. Few contemporary theories would fail to accept the probability that new pieces constantly come into being (see, e.g., Nettl 1973:5–6), even if more conservative perspectives require age as a true measure of tradition. Various forms of the compromise exist in a few theories—for example, in the distinction between individual origin and communal authorship that Sharp and Vaughan Williams make (Vaughan Williams 1954:54–58). Origin thus has both individual and communal determinants. Distinguishing many of the compromise theories is the admission that change occurs and has occurred historically. Contemporary tradition is therefore distinct from that of the past and perhaps completely unlike anything that may have existed at a point of origin. When change is accepted as a normal component of folk music tradition, any rigid conceptualization of origin necessarily becomes impossible.

Authenticity and Change

Authenticity and change are concepts that dialectically address the relation between origins and the present, emphasizing the ways in which one is reached from the other. These concepts therefore establish temporal frameworks for tradition; they provide a historical perspective. *Authenticity* in this sense can be defined as the consistent representation of the origins of a piece (or a style or a genre) in subsequent versions or at later moments in the tradition's chronology; with regard to those aspects that are salient, the piece remains the piece (cf. Karpeles 1951:14). The focus of authenticity is on the past; change, in contrast, more often focuses on the present. Authenticity need not be idealized and strictly construed, but it often is. In its most rigid forms, authenticity eschews change, or at least views it as aberrant. Authenticity tends therefore to assign primacy to the centrality and perpetuation of a particular canon (Wiora 1949:16). In the Anglo-American ballad tradition, the Child ballads constitute this sort of canon, always buttressed against defilement by unauthentic versions. Many scholars have presumed, therefore, that the Child ballads have long existed as a grouping with natural origins, and they search to discover ballads that conform to and justify the canon, even manufacturing authenticity if need be. Authenticity may also be ethnically prescribed (e.g., Saygun 1951:7). Performers, too, often search for solace in theories of authenticity that tell them how to do certain things in certain ways in order to reconstruct the authenticity of the style, that is, to play only the "original" version.

Because the acceptance of *change* focuses on the way differences arise to distinguish subsequent versions from the original, it is often the antithesis of authenticity. Preoccupation with origins and concern for a preexistent canon are often irrelevant; they may also ignore what is presumed to be reality or what is relished as vitality. Theories of change, thus, concern themselves more with processes than with the products of an earlier time. Whereas the active preservation of authentic versions may theoretically form one extreme of change, theories of change more commonly interpret the appearance of variants as inevitable, if not normative. Accordingly, the role of the individual creator is intrinsic to the customary evolution of tradition.

Change assumes many forms, some emphasizing development of the tradition, others the processes of disintegration that sometimes accompany oral tradition. Theories of folk music origins have traditionally observed three broad directions of change. The first includes various patterns of growing complexity, whether these proceed "naturally" according to evolution or accord special privilege to folk music as inspiration and melodic source for other genres (Wiora 1949:14). The opposite direction has understandably been more notorious, for it designates the upper strata of society as the source for materials worked by the folk substratum into folk music. Called *gesunkenes Kulturgut* (fallen cultural artifacts) by its architect, Hans Naumann, this theory (Naumann 1922) earned a remarkably diverse following and captured the indignant attention of many critics who spent considerable time debunking it. A third category of theories might be subsumed by the rubric *diffusion*, which demonstrates change not so much in the variation of individual pieces as in the general mobility of repertories. Individual pieces, therefore, had tremendous abilities to wander from culture to culture, regardless of place and conditions of origin (cf. Tappert 1890 and Wiora 1953). In each of these three general directions, change causes tradition to proceed progressively away from origins, rendering the depictions of those origins increasingly abstract and immaterial to the vitality of the tradition.

For those seeking to delimit the generic realm of folk music, assessing the balance between authenticity and change is often extremely important. If one believes that the true substance of folk music lies in its elements of authenticity, the unauthentic is of great danger. Ordaining the "unauthentic" is its otherness: its contrast with the aesthetic ideal of the past and its witness to the challenge of the present. When the presence of the unauthentic exhibits imbalance with the authentic, pieces cease to be folk music, crossing the border into popular music instead. As popular music, the unauthentic contributes generic characteristics of its own: a known composer, a recent composition, association with diverse and urban social functions, transmission by the mass media. The contrast with authenticity becomes ever sharper, the genesis of folk music more tautologically restrictive. Only the past can prescribe the conditions of contemporary folk music, but the past is beyond our ken. When argued in its most stringent forms, authenticity widens the gap between the past and the present, idealizing the validity of folk music's origins but purposely failing to define them.

The Dialectical Articulation of Folk Music's Origins

As the search for origins juxtaposes the past and present of folk music— harmoniously or not—it generates many of the most important dialectical considerations in the study of folk music. Not least of these considerations is the dialectic between the universality and the relativism of folk music. Does everyone have folk music? If so, is folk music then a link to the common origins of the human species, or of all culture? One might counter by asking why folk music so often exists in circumscribed repertories and delimited cultures—for example, as a genre of "national music" in some theories. If such relativism is accepted, does folk music therefore constitute a cross-cultural construct that might suggest a universal basis for polygenesis? These questions further frame the entire concept of folk music as a genre of folkloristics. To be a genre, folk music must demonstrate some commonality with regard to its origins, but that same commonality tends to idealize the genre to such extremes that individual pieces consistently fail to conform to its conditions.

Universality and relativism appear in other forms, as in the location of origins in communality or individuality. For many folk music theorists the community is the only possible setting for the origins of music. Cohesion, consciousness of the natural world, and the compulsion to share culture all underlie tradition and generate a folk spirit. But it is impossible to deny that the individual creates and engages in the generation of new songs. The dialectical relation makes clear, however, the realization that community is an aggregate of individuals. In different ways, then, communality and individuality specify that the origins are theoretically timeless, whether ubiquitous in the past or ongoing in the present.

The search for origins also suggests the dialectical relation between realism and modernism. Many theories rest on the premise that folk music imitates, but they assume a proximity to the object imitated that is made more difficult by the modernization and urbanization of society. Realism and modernism on their surfaces imply the possibility of rapprochement: the real can be modern; the modern can be real. But practice belies rapprochement when one insists that change must embody the past to be traditional.

Realism and modernism have other theoretical companions, including the relative role that oral and written tradition play in the transmission of folk music. Extreme interpretations would see realism as a means of generating oral tradition, treating realism even as a type of mnemonic device. Modernism, in contrast, makes available new techniques for facilitating transmission. In effect, oral tradition extends backward in time beyond the point of recollection, whereas written tradition arrests and redirects the flow of transmission by specifying the vehicles for individual actions. Considered together in dialectical relation, however, oral and written traditions suggest that the possibilities for folk music's origins are virtually limitless.

Is folk music art or artifice, a form of expression that is natural or one that is learned? Yet another dialectical concern results from probing the genesis of folk music to contrast its aesthetic and functional aspects. Aesthetic independence accrues to any assertion of primordial origins; if not fully expressed at the time of origin, basic aesthetic characteristics were at least immanent. Functional associations mean that folk music changes as society changes; here, too, there is a sort of aesthetic immanence in the plasticity that permits change to occur. The questions of art and artifice, of course, return one to the roles of nature that theories of origin require or ignore. If the origins of folk music ultimately rest in nature, there results a universality claiming that all people are naturally folk musicians. When all people can aspire to the performance of folk music, the need to practice, excel, or specialize diminishes, again returning us to an idealized society. In contrast, when change and the creation of new pieces result from artifice, differentiation and specialization require that certain individuals emerge as folk musicians and others only passively participate in tradition. But, of course, folk music is both art and artifice. Some musicians do stand out in tradition because of their investment of time in the learning and acquisition of specialized skills, but they cannot depart too far from the community's expectations without stepping outside the tradition. The individual musician's ability to introduce new pieces and new processes of composition necessarily benefits from the traditional models of folk music's origins held by the community. The formulation of concepts of origin—whether tenaciously holding to the past or turning to the innovation of the present—continues to undergird folk music tradition.

One may or may not believe it possible to muster enough empirical evidence to identify the origins of folk music or to discuss them in a meaningful way. Eventually, we recognize that there are pieces whose origins we can identify and those about which we can only speculate. Similarly, we may observe elements of style whose introduction into tradition can be traced to the contributions of identifiable musicians; other stylistic practices may appear immalleable over time, extending the possibility of discovering any circumstances related to their genesis far beyond the limits of available evidence. Speculation, at some level, remains a part of the search for origins.

Speculation is also a process of questioning, and the queries it raises as we endeavor to sort out the beginnings of folk music are central to the study of this genre of folklore. Just as the origins of folk music range from a mythic past to the specificity of the present, so too do concepts of folk music embrace elements of the unrealizable and the real, the intangible and the tangible. In part, folk music is an aesthetic ideal; in part, it is a functional accompaniment to basic social activity. Tradition is fashioned from both an authenticity that clings to the past and a process of change that continuously reshapes the present. That folk music is both a product of the past and a process of the present is essential to the commingling of stability and vitality, which together provide the substance and dynamism of oral tradition.

TWO

Folk Music and Oral Tradition

> Despite all that has been argued to demon-
> strate to the contrary, it is *tradition* that
> makes the folk-song a distinct *genre*, both as
> to text and music.
>
> Fannie H. Eckstorm and
> Phillips Barry (1930:2)

Oral tradition fosters both the creativity and the stability of folk music. So strong is the correlation of oral tradition with folk music that most definitions treat oral tradition as fundamental to folk music, if not its most salient feature. Oral tradition has provided many useful approaches for understanding the trans-mission of music in nonliterate societies; its dialectical relation with written tra-dition has proved equally valuable for understanding the failure of folk music to disappear in highly literate societies. Indeed, if modern scholarship has increas-ingly accepted the orality inherent in all genres of music, it has accordingly ex-panded rather than constricted our concepts of folk music in the modern world.

Oral tradition comprises both musical and ethnographic concerns essential to the study of folk music. The musical elements of oral tradition include form and style, folk taxonomies of music and indigenous systems of music theory, and perceptions of the differences and similarities that relate or distinguish individual pieces. Those aspects of music that lend themselves to memorization and those spawning elaboration determine how folk music will change or remain stable. The structure of folk music often provides the infrastructure of change and stability allowable in oral tradition. In this sense, one can speak of a musical core in the oral tradition of folk music.

Oral tradition is also a measure of a community's sense of itself, its boundaries, and the shared values drawing it together. Folk music can be a repository for these values and a voice for their expression. Oral tradition often determines the social acceptability and limitations of these values through its continuous process of sifting and winnowing. Some values gradually become stylized or vestigial; others enter and exit quickly from tradition; and still others consolidate to form a cultural core that oral tradition undergirds through many generations. Changes in a community's social structure thus influence not only its folk music repertory but also the ways in which this repertory is transmitted. Musical change reflects—indeed, becomes a metaphor for—cultural change. Together, these two types of change animate the oral tradition of folk music.

The Units of Transmission

The oral transmission of folk music depends on memory and the mnemonic devices that facilitate it. A singer learns a song by recognizing markers that he or she has used previously. Audiences also expect to encounter markers they have experienced in other songs. These markers may be small—coupling a word with a motif of a few notes—or as extensive as an entire piece. The density of these markers may be so great that accurate performance results in exact repetition of a song as the singer first experienced it; their musical function may be such that they encourage new phrase combinations or improvisation. Each repertory and each genre may have some mnemonic devices unique to it and others almost universal in distribution. Some mnemonic aids require rather sophisticated specialization, whereas others need no more than naive repetition. Taken as a whole, these memory markers become the units of transmission that make oral tradition possible.

Music is itself one of the most effective mnemonic devices in oral tradition (Vansina 1985:46). The rhythm and syntax of melody can reinforce those of a text. Melodic closure may occur simultaneously with textual closure. The form of a musical stanza will very often conform to a textual stanza. If text and movement have particular ritual functions, music can elaborate and stylize those functions, thereby heightening the participatory possibilities for an entire community. The mnemonic effectiveness of music is perhaps best illustrated by the difficulty experienced by anyone trying to recall the words of a favorite song divorced from its melody; at best, only a severely compromised version results. Music abounds in those parameters that animate oral tradition. Rhythm, because of its biological basis, is one of the clearest examples of such a parameter (Ong 1982:35), but its potential for symmetry and even mimesis may even serve to enhance oral tradition.

The largest unit in the oral transmission of folk music is the piece—the song, the dance, that musical entity to which a culture ascribes a specific name. The piece of music usually contains internal mnemonic devices, but its total form also serves as a unit in transmission. Not least among the ways it serves transmission is its definition of performance or its summary and closure of narrative. Pieces contrast in structure, function, and length in different genres or cultures.

A ballad reconstructs a discrete narrative by means of fairly repetitive stanzas; the larger narrative drama of epic is punctuated by numerous small episodes with continual reshaping by formulaic and improvisatory structures. But the performance of each constitutes a piece. The narrative of both lends itself to identification with a name, and the music likewise lends itself to analysis of formal unity.

Smaller elements give rise to the structural integrity of a piece. The relative centrality of these elements in different traditions also contributes to such factors as stability, change, and distribution within a culture. If the units of transmission are relatively large, change often proceeds more slowly than in a genre with numerous small units. Iterative form, such as stanzaic or stichic (line-by-line) composition, relies on the memorization of textual units with repetitive rhythmic and metric patterns, frequently combined with other poetic devices, such as rhyme. The musical organization of the stanza and line also stabilizes their transmission. Musical organization usually enhances textual patterns. The more the patterns of music and text complement each other, the more a song's form facilitates memory (Vansina 1985:16).

In some genres of folk music, the musical and textual markers operate at a much smaller level. The general designation for such markers is *formula*, but one also encounters such terms as *convention, motif,* or *phrase* with roughly equivalent usages. Formulae appear in most genres of folk music, although in some they are primarily responsible for the generation of overall form. Of varying sizes, formulae are larger than the smallest structural units in folk music (Ong 1982:36). They usually combine several smaller units to create a larger one that is thereby more memorable. In Anglo-American ballads, "hand" becomes a formula when preceded by "lily-white," and names become formulaic when appended to a qualifier—for example, "Sweet William." Textual and musical formulae often initiate and close stanzas or lines, thus acting as framing devices to articulate overall form (Abrahams and Foss 1968:33). Formulae may have an integrity quite separate from that of the individual piece. They may, for example, appear in different pieces or in the folk music of different cultures. They may behave like entire tunes with regard to change and transmission, but they are not performed in isolation outside the context of the larger piece of which they are one formulaic component (Nettl 1983:111).

In some oral traditions, formula has acquired a considerable degree of integrity itself, perhaps more than entire songs. That may be the case in Yugoslav epics, whose intensive study by Milman Perry, Albert B. Lord, and others has yielded the oral-formulaic theory. This theory recognizes tremendous stability in small formulae, with wide-ranging variation and creativity in the performance of the entire epic. The "piece," then, is really the composite of many performances, and one could not properly speak of the transmission of an entire piece as a discrete entity (Lord 1960:125). The long Yugoslav epics—sometimes containing thousands of lines—are an extreme example of formula, but they illustrate the dual role formula plays as a mnemonic device and a catalyst for creativity. So important is this role that some scholars measure the extent of orality in a folk music tradition by the prevalence of formulaic structures (ibid.:130, and Kleeman 1985–86:21).

Does the piece then constitute a unit for analysis? Is it a text that we can subject to critical examination? Just what does a recording of "Es klappert die Mühle am rauschenden Bach" (The mill wheel splashes in the rushing stream) from the rural Midwest represent? Both indigenous and critical responses suggest that it is appropriate to treat the piece as a text, but one inseparable from a context of performance and tradition. Thus, analysis of a single song stands not just to proffer a hermeneutic explanation of its form or the meaning of its text, but to illumine its relation to the entire tradition of which it is a part. The text exists only within a context of performance and tradition, and it is one task of the student of folk song to understand how text, performance, and tradition interrelate (cf. Vansina 1985:33–34).

To think of the piece as somehow "authentic" or even archetypal is to treat it as a text in the most restricted sense, that is, as isolated from performance and tradition. A Midwestern version of "Es klappert die Mühle am rauschenden Bach" can be analyzed to elucidate form and structure, but if one fails to see beyond its text, one fails also to question why a German folk song should exist in oral tradition in the Midwest, or what community would maintain such a tradition and how it could do so. One fails to consider, moreover, what changes may have occurred in this tradition as the outside forces influencing it grew increasingly different from those in Germany or in other communities of immigrant Germans. These questions suggest the need always to compare and contrast the individual unit of transmission, the piece, with the processes of change that render any individual piece in myriad versions. This interrelation of product and process—of musical text and cultural change—generates a dialectic essential to the oral tradition of folk music.

The Process of Change

Earlier theories of folk music transmission often stressed its putative sameness and stability. A folk musician was thought to perform each song exactly as he or she had learned it. The predominant motivation of the performer was to replicate and reproduce, to minimize self-expression in order to let "the piece speak for itself" (Abrahams and Foss 1968:201). When such theories reckoned with change, it was frequently to account for the multiple variants that most collections or regions contained. Imperfect memory was the culprit: variants resulted not because of intentional creativity, but because nonliterate musicians introduced errors and alteration. Change thus resulted from "the tricks which memory will play" (Barry 1933:4).

This view of folk music transmission portrays a very conservative process of change. It is likely that there are cultures in which extreme replicability is the ultimate value motivating oral tradition, but there are few cultures in which some form of change is completely unacceptable. There are other oral cultures in which individual creativity is highly valued and society judges musicians on their ability to render each version of a song unique. Preservation for its own sake may be relatively unknown in such societies. Audiences may judge performances according to the novelty that they sense, rather than the accuracy of rendition.

Cultural attitudes toward stability and change differ vastly. In most cultures, stability and change coexist, one perhaps more prevalent but seldom pushing out the other. Attitudes differ, too, according to the particular aspects of oral tradition that become the foci of concerns about stability and change. Some groups—the Amish in North America, for example—equate change with encroachment from the outside; others identify a rather stable core, such as the corpus of motifs and modal concepts constituting the Persian *radif,* which, even when learned from printed forms, permits considerable variation and improvisation during performance (cf. Barkechli 1963, Massoudieh 1978, and Nettl and Foltin 1972).

The musical elements of different oral traditions also lend themselves to stability and change in multifarious ways. Those traditions that concentrate stability in small, formulaic units may allow considerable improvisation and creativity in larger units. The transmission of certain genres requires memorization of larger units, and there may be very little tolerance for change during performance. The level and density of memorization may retard or accelerate change. Some processes of memorization even function in a dynamic way, as in the process labeled "scanning" by Jan Vansina, whereby memory works "according to the sequence of accession" (1985:43). Thus, the sequence of events in a narrative genre of folk song must unfold along a logical timeline. A lapse in memory or a deleted phrase could jumble the story so that it ceased to make sense, signaling a collapse in narrative structure that might eventually transform the piece into a completely different genre, such as lyric folk song.

Even within a single musical culture there are pieces that change very little and others that spawn remarkably diverse variants. To describe the range and tolerance of change occurring within musical cultures in such a way that oral traditions might be examined comparatively, Bruno Nettl has proposed four models of the history through which individual pieces may pass (Nettl 1982:8–9). Stability predominates in his type I: "the composition, once created, may be carried on without change, more or less intact" (ibid.:8). Change in Nettl's type II is fairly regular and produces variants according to alterations of a similar nature; change follows a more or less predictable path. Different quantities and degrees of change occur in type III; a single version may eventually produce many variants, some of them very similar to the original, others resembling it not at all. Type IV is not much different from type III, except in the propensity of pieces to absorb new material as they change; new versions rather quickly become unlike the original, even when absorption of external material assumes predictable patterns (ibid.:9).

Comparison of Nettl's third and fourth types raises another question: How do a society's concepts of similarity and difference affect the oral tradition of folk music? The processes of change in types III and IV are in essence the same. In type III, however, prolificacy results from internal alterations, whereas in type IV it comes from external borrowing. Do the variants in type III therefore demonstrate greater similarity than those in type IV just because the history of type III is more self-contained? Are the variants of type IV more different because of their external origin, perhaps leading some to insist that the variants are actually completely new pieces? Such questions may serve to confuse the issues that surround the identification of stability and change in oral tradition, for they clearly show that it is not easy to make an immediate claim for stability against change, or vice versa. They also illustrate the extent to which these issues are interrelated. Stability does not exist in a conceptual universe divorced from change. It is only through an understanding of a society's own concepts of this dialectic of oral tradition that one can perceive the ways the units of folk music relate to or differ from each other.

A remarkable range of cultural, musical, and psychological factors animates and stems the processes of change in oral tradition. Whereas theories of folk music transmission stressing replication attribute change to flaws in perception or memory, it seems more likely that a number of factors combine to forge the direction of change. Psychological factors inevitably have ramifications in musical structure; cultural factors may lead to specific psychological attitudes toward change. Any typology of the processes of change in oral tradition can be only tentative, at least insofar as it isolates processes that function in a concerted rather than an isolated way. The typology that follows here is thus offered as a group of concepts that frequently characterize the musical change that folk music undergoes. Although a few processes have a propensity for operating with certain other processes, the typology intentionally lacks a hierarchy. The boundaries between processes, while hypothetically identifiable, are most often fluctuating and murky.

Both the positive and the negative impacts of memory on oral tradition are obvious in the processes designated here as repetition and forgetting. *Repetition* as a process depends on formulae, but when portrayed in the light of change, it is a good deal more complicated. Repetition also describes the replacement of one musical phrase with another, more memorable phrase, as when the four-line stanza ABBC becomes ABBA or ABCD becomes ABCA. A similar type of repetition occurs on a larger scale, as when related events in a narrative folk song are given the same musical setting. Scholars refer to this type of repetition as "incremental," imputing to it the dramatic function of leading up to and then heightening the climax of narrative folk song (Barry 1933:5 and Abrahams and Foss 1968:33). Repetition tends either to crystallize and strengthen the formulae underpinning a particular version or to cause such extensive proliferation that formula actually replaces other structures necessary for the articulation of more complicated genres; an example of such replacement is the elimination of dramatic impetus in narrative folk song, leaving in its stead lyrical folk song.

The obverse of repetition and reliance on formulae is *forgetting*. German scholarship has referred to the degeneration and disintegration of folk song with resulting new versions as *Zersingen*, or "singing into bits and pieces" (Danckert 1966:30–36, Dessauer 1928, and Goja 1920). During the past half century, the self-destructive quality of *Zersingen* has caused it to fall from favor. I purposely use *forgetting* because of its more neutral tenor and broader, cross-cultural applicability. The imperfection of memory can engender both creativity and degeneration, depending on the cultural attitudes toward change. It therefore behooves one not to think of forgetting as simply the lopping off of salient members from the body of a piece, eventually reducing it to a desiccated and lifeless trunk. Forgetting also results from mishearing or lack of understanding (Abrahams and Foss 1968:17), or even from mistakes during performance (Nettl 1983:105). Mistakes naturally cause the appearance of new textual and musical phrases, sometimes only distorting the meaning or form of a previous version but often engendering new versions that take on a life of their own.

The stabilized unit of folk music in oral tradition is often a fusion of several versions rather than being a single, original version. The process producing this stabilized unit is called *consolidation*. Consolidation may take place in overt ways, such as *borrowing* from other pieces, or in more covert ways, such as the *assimilation* of like melodic phrases. One of the most overt paths of consolidation has been dubbed by Nettl the " 'Top of Old Smoky' effect" to describe the creation of new versions in ways similar to those occurring when the broadside ballad "The Pretty Mohea" adapted for its second half the popular country tune "On Top of Old Smoky" (Nettl 1983:108). Whether this particular act of borrowing was conscious on the part of the communities where "The Pretty Mohea" was traditional is not known. The borrowing of a well-known tune for new texts, as in broadside ballads, or even for other texts long a part of traditional singing, as in vernacular hymn-singing traditions of German-American immigrants, is a long-standing practice (Bohlman 1985:38–40).

Consolidation may be a gradual process of change, or it may occur dramatically to precipitate and then to stabilize a new style. The formation of Native American musical styles that embraced numerous tribal groups from different areas has demonstrated both rates of consolidation. The development of a pan-Plains style has occurred more gradually, finding new catalysts in changing social settings for music-making, such as the powwow, whose explicit purpose draws diverse tribal and communal groups together. The most notable case of rapid consolidation was the emergence of Ghost Dance music in the late nineteenth century. In this style, probably derived initially from the music of Native American tribes in the Great Basin area, phrases occurred in pairs, the ,second often an exact or near repetition of the first (example 1). The consolidated style made it possible for Ghost Dance music to spread quickly to many areas of the American West.

Consolidation of musical style not infrequently allows particular songs or genres to pass into the oral tradition of several communities. Musical style thus can combine different musical traits in such a way that its foreignness subsides, or at least becomes inconsequential. The Spanish romance, with its eight-syllable lines and four-line stanzas, spread throughout Latin America during the centuries after the initial Spanish settlement because of this type of adaptability, which in turn led both to well-preserved forms and to those with considerable variation and structural change (Olsen 1980:389–91). Hiromi Lorraine Sakata observed this pattern of stylistic consolidation during the late 1960s and early 1970s when the folk song "Mullā Mohammed Jān" (example 2), which originated in the city of Herat, became widespread in Afghanistan and had even been recorded in Iran. The formulaic structure of the second half of each line and the repetitiveness of the refrain served both to popularize the song and to give singers "the opportunity to improvise short, appropriate rhyming phrases without worrying about a difficult melody or strict poetic rhythm" (Sakata 1983:145). Consolidation may have been, in effect, a function of a simplified style, yet a style that simultaneously contributed to the creativity requisite for quickening oral tradition.

Two patterns of musical and textual change often initiate consolidation and borrowing. The first pattern retains the formal superstructure of a piece. *Substitution* takes place within the piece, often affecting units smaller than the musical or textual phrase. One type of substitution occurs when commonplace

Wanagi Wacipi Olowan

Singer: Tatanka-Ptecila (Short Bull)
♩ = 144 mm
With spirit, in moderate
Source: Curtis 1907:66

Pine Ridge, South Dakota
Collected and transcribed
by Natalie Curtis

I - na, he - ku - ye, I - na, he - ku - ye,

Mi - šun - ka - la ce - ya - ya o - ma - ni - yi,

Mi - šun - ka - la ce - ya - ya o - ma - ni - yi

I - na, he - ku - ye, I - na, he - ku - ye,

A - te he - ye - lo, A - te - he - ye - lo!

Translation

Mother, O come back, Mother, O come back,
Little brother calls as he seeks thee, weeping,
Little brother calls as he seeks thee, weeping,
Mother, O come back, Mother, O come back,
Saith the Father, Saith the Father!

Example 1

references replace those less well known in the community. Roger D. Abrahams and George Foss have observed that such substitutions tend to reflect a community's sense of either the universal or the local (1968:29–31). Thus the outsiders portrayed in many Middle Eastern folk genres frequently shed all traces of unique identity, acting instead according to a universal and hackneyed role that gypsies, Jews, or other outsiders are imagined to play with stereotypical regularity, regardless of whether such groups could possibly have played such a role. Substitution of local names for stranger foreign names is a common way of drawing a folk song closer to the canonic core of a community.

Addition of borrowed or new material to the piece's superstructure is another impetus to consolidation. Samuel P. Bayard's exploration of the history of the tune he labels "The Job of Journeywork" revealed certain stages at which shortened versions of the tune were expanded by adding material from external

Mullā Mohammed Jān

Singer: Zainab
Sorna: Mohammed Omar
Source: Sakata 1983:144–45

Herat, Afghanistan
Transcribed by
Hiromi Lorraine Sakata

Translation (H. L. Sakata)

Come, let's go to Mazar,   Mulla Mohammed Jan
To see the wild tulips,   oh, dear sweetheart
We will cry around   Sakhi Jan's shrine.

I saw you from afar,   Mulla Mohammed Jan
I saw you were happy,   oh, dear sweetheart
At last I will get you,   oh, dear sweetheart.

EXAMPLE 2

sources (Bayard 1954:13–33 and Nettl 1983:105–8). It is theoretically possible that this process of shortening, coupled with addition, can continue beyond the point at which variants contain any remnants of the original tune, even though the history has been one of continual and logical change.

Creativity as a motivation for change in folk music has both individual and communal roots. By far, most theoretical discussions and personalized visions of folk music have stressed the communal underpinnings of change. Jacob Grimm's enjoinder *"das Volk dichtet"* has persisted in various forms to the present. It is, nonetheless, probable that many of the changes introduced into folk tradition result from acts of *individual creativity,* some of which may be accidental but others intentional and idiosyncratic. One locus for the role of the individual is in the act of composition itself. Improvisatory genres require relatively more individual creativity than those for which the community would frown upon improvisation. Composition has widely varying meanings when applied to folk music. It may refer to the creation of a new piece; it may refer to the publication of a broadsheet, necessarily tied to existing tunes and textual formulae even if its narrative is new; it may refer to the conscious performance of unique variants. Nettl suggests that a useful distinction between individual and communal creativity lies in the history of individual songs and versions (1973:5). The first stage, composition, relies predominantly on individual acts. Thereafter, it may be *communal re-creation*—the gradual and accepted reworking of songs by individuals other than the original creators—that determines the pattern of change. Communal re-creation has become a tried-and-true concept of folk music transmission since its formulation as a theory by Phillips Barry (1933).

The efficacy of communal re-creation is a consequence of musical and cultural factors, but clearly the question of widespread acceptance—change permissible within canonical strictures—is central to it. Communal re-creation comprises many considerations necessary for assessment of the different processes of change presented here. It weighs the role of the individual against that of the community and does so without negating either. It accepts change as the creative and natural result of the history of folk music in oral tradition, yet recognizes the checks that a community places on the direction of change. And it combines cultural and musical motivations for the composition and preservation of folk music. Communal re-creation, as well as the other types of change it subsumes, stresses the dynamic quality of folk music by dialectically counterpoising the products and processes of oral tradition. Indeed, it is this broad-ranging ability to explain musical change against a backdrop of stability that causes one to concur with Nettl's claim that "this process, called 'communal re-creation,' is one of the things that distinguish folk music from other kinds" (1973:5).

The Dialectic of Oral Tradition

The dialectic of oral tradition consists of both products and the processes by which these products are derived. For folk music, the product is the discrete entity—the song, the record of a single performance, a version of the unit of transmission—whereas the process is the continuation of transmission. This process theoretically has beginning and ending points and therefore comprises all renderings of the product. Product and process are not so simple as creation and inscription of text, for each of the dialectical components extends to and represents other aspects of oral tradition. Some of these aspects derive from the music itself, others from its cultural context. Interpreted in relation to the dialectic of product and process, however, these components of oral tradition reflect the dynamic force inherent in the performance, transmission, and reception of folk music (cf. Vansina 1985:3–5).

In every repertory of folk music there is a balance between characteristics that many pieces share and those that distinguish pieces from each other. In other words, one can identify elements of unity and uniqueness that together define the relation between the musical core and the boundaries of a repertory. Similarly, these characteristics represent the repertory's capacity for both collective and individual expression. Various terms have been employed to describe the interaction of these characteristics, among which *style* and *content* (e.g., Nettl 1982:10) and Saussure's *langue* and *parole* (1966) are the most common. If the coupling of these concepts suggests the unity and uniqueness within a repertory, it also frames the range within which the repertory's performance or execution—the processes yielding the products of the repertory—take place. The performative processes are by definition dynamic, constantly stating and restating the relation of content to style, *parole* to *langue* (cf. Austin 1975). They are therefore also constantly responsive to and expressive of cultural pressures that effect change.

Performance of folk music draws upon both the unity and the uniqueness of the tradition. Depending on the cultural expectations available to the performer and the audience, each performance combines elements of unifying style with individualizing content. In some cultural settings, the expectation requires that unity predominate; in others, the tolerance of individuality is greater. Whatever the cultural constraints and expectations, performance of folk music brings content and style into immediate contact with each other. The individual choices necessary in each performance continually restate the dialectic that defines a tradition and repertory of folk music, while ensuring that they are in a state of constant change (Nettl 1983:108–9).

Contrasting the relative components of tradition and transmission has often provided another means of addressing the dialectic of unity and uniqueness in folk music. Again, tradition as the sum of all individual performances is shaped by the processes of change, whereas the unit of transmission, the performed version of a piece, is the product marking various stages of these processes. Tradition, moreover, acquires the dynamism of history; it has an essentially diachronic nature. Because it can denote a particular moment in tradition's temporality, transmission approximates synchrony. For the individual performer, individual performance is always a synchronic act: his or her version of a folk song is the correct one, and it therefore epitomizes the entire tradition (Barry 1933:4). For the community, however, the entire history of a folk music repertory, whether known to the community's members or not, comprises the tradition (Nettl 1982:3).

Stability and change exist in both community and individual constructs of tradition and transmission. The correctness that the individual presumes in his or her correct version exudes a confidence in stability; nevertheless, it is exactly such an individualized stability that reflects change when any "correct" version is compared with all other versions. Contrastingly, the expansiveness of community tradition is itself an assurance of stability, but only because of its ability to encompass widespread and ongoing change within its various repertories.

Historiographic consideration of various folk music theories reveals very different concepts of the interaction of stability and change in transmission. One of the earliest models, Wilhelm Tappert's "wandering melodies" (1890), attributed remarkable integrity to individual melodies. This integrity was so great that motifs from individual melodies presumably could and often did travel from region to region, regardless of physical and political impediments (cf. Nettl 1983:104). Many melodies could withstand the ravages of time with a stability so great "that their existence is almost as old as history itself" (Tappert 1890:5). Implicit in Tappert's claims for stability is the changeability of tradition vis-à-vis the units of transmission that constitute it, although he was not particularly concerned with applying that changeability to melodies whose integrity was not quite so intrepid as the world travelers in his model.

Melodic integrity is also primary in most concepts of tune families and tune histories. In the tune family, stability results from the sharing of stylistic—one might say genetic—traits. There are inevitably other traits that are not shared, and it is these that explain variation and change. Still, it is the stability of family relationships that provides the soil to nurture the family tree from which the limbs of variation spring. Tune histories, too, are initially determined according to the sharing of melodic traits, but these histories are the products of both internal and external forces. In other words, the stability and change represented by each piece of music are components of an entire repertory, which in turn sustains or fails to sustain the life of the piece (Coffin 1961:248–50 and McMillan 1964:305–6).

Just as stability often resides in some form in the pieces constituting a repertory, so too is it evident in the processes of transmission. Transmission may be determined not just by what pieces of music are put together but by how they are put together. Style is one of the primary determinants of the ways in which new pieces are composed or existing pieces acquire new versions. Extending the notion of style to a community's repertory, one might explain similarities by noting the stylistic penchant to create pieces of music in analogous ways. George List has applied this concept to even larger cultural areas, such as Europe, in order to explain the frequency with which certain melodic types are found in different repertories (List 1978).

The transmission of style depends in part on culture-based stability. It may also depend on the stability of structural units in folk music. Several types of folk music contain specific lines or motifs that serve as the loci of change. The "bridge" in many American popular songs functions in this way, especially when performed in improvisatory genres like jazz; Nettl has observed that this is also the case in the third line of many Czech folk songs with the form AABA (1983:111). The stability of smaller units of such repertories permits change in the larger units, thereby making the speed and direction of transmission consequences of stability and change.

How do the various components of stability and change actually fit together to form the dialectic of folk music in oral tradition? Do they all influence the direction of tradition in the same way? Even in different cultural settings? Any change, no matter how small and whether related primarily to process or product, exerts some effect on the entire repertory of which it is a part. The resulting impact and resonance of any given change must reflect the density of a repertory and the dynamics of change, again to borrow concepts proposed by Nettl (1982:11). The greater the density of a repertory, the greater the possibilities for stability. Density can be both a synchronic and a diachronic concept; that is, it can have both spatial and historical facets. The difference between the two facets is similar to Eckstorm and Barry's consideration of "tradition in space" and "tradition in time" (1930:2). If the density of tradition is quite sparse, maintaining stability may be very difficult; similarly, if the dynamics of change are very rapid, stability may be a rather insignificant factor in determining the integrity of a tradition.

Cultural attitudes constantly temper the balance between the two processes. Awareness of a sparse census of folk songs, for example, may heighten a community's endeavors to preserve or revive, producing concomitant forms of stabilization. Such endeavors may drastically alter the dynamics of change, thus transforming the entire dialectical relation between process and product. But variation in density of repertory and dynamics of change is vital to the nature of oral tradition, for it is such variation that persistently situates both stability and change in the transmission of folk music.

Oral Tradition and Written Tradition

Of the various ways of stabilizing change in oral tradition, none is more effective than written tradition. I hope the reader will bear with me when I state the coexistence of oral and written traditions as a blatant paradox, but I do so for two fundamental reasons. First, oral traditions of folk music are no longer immune from some aspect of literacy, whether it be a literacy that bears directly on folk music itself or literacy in other types of expressive behavior. Second, written traditions of folk music rely on many of the same structures and functions that make possible the oral transmission of music: formulae, iterative structure, cultural license for creativity, requisites for stability (cf. Saussure 1966:15–17). Literacy has become one of the most consistent contexts for folk music in oral tradition.

Although some scholars have insisted upon oral transmission as a prerequisite for folk music, many others have recognized the correlation of orality and literacy in the transmission of folk music (Seeger 1949–50). Barry consistently accounted for written traditions as the second of his two "media for transmission of folk-song," the other being the singer (1914:67). Barry's consideration of written tradition had a purely descriptive premise: Anglo-American folk songs in the early decades of the twentieth century circulated widely as broadsides or in chapbooks and newspapers. His descriptive premise suggests further that oral tradition and written tradition tend to be construed as ideal and somehow pure forms of transmission. But it is more likely that the history of a folk song exists sometimes in oral tradition and sometimes in written tradition, usually, however, drawing upon both. Indeed, the interaction of the two may succeed in stabilizing that history, while also facilitating and directing its change.

Written traditions also provide a frequent mode for the introduction of new folk songs into a repertory or effective conduits for external influences, if not borrowing from other repertories. Broadsides or broadsheets best exemplify the creation of new folk songs in Euro-American traditions (e.g., Shepard 1962 and Wright and Wright 1983). A composer of broadside songs writes a text, often about an event recently of concern to a community, which is then printed along with the name of one or several well-known melodies that would ade-

FIGURE 1. German-language broadside about an 1838 flood in Budapest. The name of the melody for the new song appears below the woodcut. The first verse is at the bottom. (Source: Schmidt 1970:appendix 9.)

quately set the new text. Even with the first performance, the broadside song (figure 1) stands with one foot in written tradition and the other in oral, and subsequent performances tend rather quickly to shift the song more or less completely into oral tradition.

Literary representation of music serves as a link between the musical activities in many other social settings and the oral tradition of folk music. The songs of the popular theater and of protest movements and the hymns of religious groups may be transformed into folk music after initial publication in written formats. This process of transformation is, not surprisingly, prevalent in societies or cultural settings where literacy is fairly widespread, such as Central Europe or urban centers. German scholarship has even applied the methodological category *Volksgesang* as distinguished from *Volkslied* (both are commonly translated as "folk song," but *Volksgesang* implies the change and preshaping of folk song through performance) to describe the movement of a folk music repertory from the literate boundaries to the oral core of a tradition (Schmidt 1970).

Comparison of oral and written traditions of folk music suggests that they differ more in degree than in kind. Oral tradition relies more on memory and therefore contains more repetitive patterns and the mnemonic role of formula. Stylization is often greater in oral tradition, and so is the dramatic continuity of narrative genres. Oral traditions require somewhat greater density of performance, whereas density in written traditions is a factor of the circulation and availability of texts. Because of its greater dependence on performance for maintaining the vitality of a repertory, oral tradition relies on the transmission of rather complete versions. In contrast, literate transmission often deletes some component of completeness—for example, the melody of broadside songs or refrains after the appearance of the first stanza. This difference in the completeness of the unit of transmission often effects major changes in a tradition when literate transmission begins to predominate. The emergence of printed texts in the Yugoslav epic tradition during the early twentieth century not only took the form of abbreviated printed texts but also brought about considerable thematic streamlining and the gradual collapse of formulaic structure in oral performance (Lord 1960:130–32).

It is virtually impossible in the twentieth century to discover folk music traditions that are purely oral or exclusively literate. And still another lesson has accompanied the twentieth century: the spread of various forms of literacy throughout the world has not been the death knell of folk music that some scholars have alleged. It becomes increasingly necessary, in fact, to expand our understanding of the range spanned by such concepts as orality and literacy, especially when electronic and other media of transmission exert a growing influence on folk music. The essential issue for the study of folk music is therefore not *either* oral *or* written, but the dynamics and direction of change inherent in the coexistence of these two aspects of tradition.

Oral Tradition and the Canon

The oral tradition of folk music depends on a canonic core that encapsulates stability and change. The repertories embodied by this core differ from community to community, and the processes that shape the core are different in each culture. The canonic core consists of musical and cultural, textual and contextual elements. Among the musical elements serving as the core's infrastructure are the integral units of transmission: pieces, formulae, normative settings of texts, shared musical vocabularies. The relative roles of composition, improvisation, and communal re-creation also determine what musical elements constitute the core. Cultural context is reflected in the superstructure or boundaries of the canonic core and therefore plays an active role in making each tradition distinct and characteristic of the group maintaining it. Some cultural contexts may undergird the stability of tradition by, for example, enhancing ritual or the epic recounting of collective history, while others may stimulate change by serving as the voice of protest or mediating class stratification (Lomax 1968:6).

Oral tradition reflects the selectivity of the community that initiates and bears it. It is thus not a random pattern of aesthetic and social expression but takes its shape from the stylistic concerns and emotional core of a given community. The selectivity central to oral tradition shapes its canon from the very inception of tradition and then continually reshapes it throughout the tradition's history. Items enter the canon because they somehow stand out and are worthy of special artistic attention and because they can be fitted to the tradition without sacrificing the integrity of the item or the tradition (Vansina 1985:20). The same qualities that draw items into the canon assume new functions that were once a part of oral tradition, broadening context or transforming text into mnemonic devices, for example, and thus enlivening the tradition through their stabilizing impact.

The interaction of canonic core and its boundaries bestows to the oral tradition of folk music a dynamic, variegating quality. Change and differing attitudes toward change occupy the boundary areas some distance from the core. Performance practices that produce stability have a greater density near the core of the tradition, whereas those little encouraged by audience consensus shift increasingly away from the core. In a society where individual performance is not highly valued, the boundaries of oral tradition may provide a locus for individual creativity. Change in the canon then results as some pieces of folk music move from the boundary toward the core, there perhaps to gain gradual approval from the community, for whom the piece becomes a staple in the folk music repertory (Nettl 1982:4).

The dialectic between canonic core and boundary accounts for both the stability necessary if a folk music tradition is to have meaning for a community and the changeability required to withstand, encourage, or transform influences outside the community. Folk music manifests characteristics that are both unique to a community and shared almost universally with other communities. The mitigating role of the dialectic between core and boundary also allows for this seeming contradiction. The canon of folk music in oral tradition, far from being unchanging, is fully capable of absorbing new repertory and cultural functions, albeit only after they have been transformed by the canon's boundaries into texts and contexts appropriate to the aesthetic and social criteria of the community at its core. The formation and maintenance of the canon, therefore, are predicated on stability and change, both of which are ongoing and inseparable forces in the determination of the oral tradition of folk music.

THREE

Classification: The Discursive Boundaries of Folk Music

> I believe that there are . . . collections
> with similar overall characters from different
> countries and eras, so that the question of the
> most appropriate classification systems for
> folk melodies will remain, in spite of every-
> thing, one of the most important that musical
> scholars debate and discuss together.
>
> Ilmari Krohn (1907:74)

> Any system of classification, however, is
> merely a means. The study of a melody *be-
> gins* after it has been placed in some system
> or index; it does not end there.
>
> George Herzog (1937:55)

Folk music has often demonstrated a peculiar resistance to systematic classification—or, stated more accurately, to classification systems. Despite the plethora of efforts to discern, describe, and ascribe order in folk music, classification
has often been a culture-specific or repertory-specific endeavor. The systematic
description of one repertory, no matter how much tolerance for variation it
permits, rarely extends to other repertories. Even when classification systems
are modified to account for some aspects of universality, it is usually the accuracy
of the specific that suffers, while only a few more repertories yield themselves
to the revised descriptive schemes. The history of classification therefore challenges many of the claims to the universality of folk music. At the same time,
this history consistently validates and reexamines the boundaries that regional,
local, or small-group cultures fashion for folk music. Thus, the resistance of folk
music to classification is not necessarily symptomatic of an absence of order or
unsystematic musical behavior; rather, it may better serve to illumine those
levels at which interrelated repertories and social structures prevail. When

directed toward such goals, classification stands to establish and articulate the discursive boundaries of folk music.

Classification is a metaphor for our attempts to understand and describe folk music in an orderly fashion. As an abstraction of our concepts of folk music, classification ideally should provide the infrastructure for a systematic discourse about folk music. Two problems, appearing in two general approaches to classification, often prevent this ideal from being the case, thereby limiting also the effectiveness of the systematic discourse. Many inductive approaches begin by describing the specific and then base their theoretical models on that. Whether the specific is musical, cultural, or ideological in nature, its limits become the limitations of the theoretical model. Deductive approaches, in contrast, begin by prescribing a model and then determining which aspects from different repertories fit the model. Both of these approaches frequently result in a fixing and ossification of the canon, which leads to a seductiveness that may underlie classification. We observe this seductiveness when fieldworkers return from a collecting trip ready to make claims for the persistence of this or that canon, even while a sturdy defense against encroachment from other, usually more modern or popular, repertories shows signs of weakening.

Attempts to classify folk music face some confounding paradoxes. Even though classification is most unequivocal when it takes on specific parameters of folk music, it is limited unless it also examines the interrelations of all parameters, some of which are only vaguely understood. Similarly, there are the occurrences of variations and exceptions; to what extent can we recognize and account for them before they undermine even the broadest classification system? Hardly surprising, then, is the frequency with which classification systems have concentrated on only one aspect of folk music—tune or text separately, say, or music devoid of social and historical context. How can one instead account for questions of transmission, origins, musical structure and form, text and tune interaction, and the formation of repertories? These issues are, of course, broadly representative of folk music study in general. By looking more closely at classification, both historically and analytically, we concentrate these issues, providing them with a forum so that they might shed light on each other. That, too, is what the best classification systems achieve.

Genres of and Approaches to Classification

Scholars engaged in classification have devoted primary attention to the products of folk music, relegating processes to a position of secondary importance. Most systems have therefore arranged and ordered the individual pieces constituting a large, presumably coherent repertory. Because the earliest classifiers in the nineteenth and early twentieth centuries worked from collections and were themselves often not collectors, they had little evidence at their disposal concerning processes of change or social function. Through classification they hoped to achieve two ends. First, they hoped to devise a way of gaining easy access to and identifying the individual pieces in large collections. Second, they sought ways to define the interrelation of items in large collections, usually motivated by historical and nationalistic considerations. The nature of these goals necessitated an approach that concentrated initially on specific items and then expanded to broader levels of comparability. Accordingly, the early classifiers concerned themselves more with the establishment of repertory boundaries than with analytical approaches that would allow for exploration beyond such boundaries.

The first attempts to classify relied on song texts; melody received relatively little attention until the twentieth century (Herzog 1937:49, Mosely 1964:9, and Sorce Keller 1984:100). As a criterion of classification, song texts permitted a fair degree of specific identification: dialect could locate the text geographically and subject matter presumably established function. Many of the early classifiers were linguists whose primary concerns lay with the explication of textual matters. Many early collections of English folk song reflected this textual impetus. *The English and Scottish Popular Ballads* by Francis James Child (1882–98) contained texts only. Not only were melodies lacking, but the classification system that later became formalized as the "Child ballads" was arrived at completely on the basis of textual subject matter. So entrenched was this early method of classification according to text that subsequent attempts to classify Anglo-American ballads have simply accepted it, in essence working around it when ascribing tune types to the narrative structure of the ballads (cf. Seeger 1966 and Kolinski 1968 and 1969). German anthologies employed a somewhat different approach to classification by text, incorporating aspects of social function together with more standard literary typologies. Thus, the genres identified in the three-volume *Deutscher Liederhort* (Erk 1893–94) included such categories as "songs of departure and wandering" and "historical-political songs" as well as "ballads" and the "songs of legends." This mixture of literary, functional, and contemporary genres has persisted in German classification systems and is basic to the broad conceptualization of genre that characterizes German folk music scholarship today (cf. Brednich, et al. 1973 and 1975 and Bausinger 1980:263–94).

Melodic classification began in earnest somewhat later than textual approaches for both practical and intellectual reasons. Even in collections that included musical aspects, notation was indefinite or was modified by anthologizers to suit practical ends, as in arrangements in harmonized versions for choral performance. Many collectors, moreover, possessed only a modicum of musical skills, which prevented them from transcribing musical aspects during fieldwork—a difficult enough task for anyone before the advent of sound-recording devices, when transcriptions often required repeated performances or reliance on the collector's memory.

As collections grew larger, the need for musical classification became more pressing. The early architects of classification responded to two primary motivations. The first resulted from the need for easy access to large collections. The second sought to interpret the ways in which the melodies of large collections were related to each other. The first comprehensive attempt to incorporate these two methods appeared in articles by Oswald Koller (1902–3) and Ilmari Krohn (1902–3; cf. also Nettl 1983:120). Koller proposed a means of locating a tune among many others when—and only when—one knows the exact pitch complement. Krohn devised a means of abstracting tunes so that many tunes might be compared to discover patterns of relationship. Koller's approach was primarily lexicographic: one could easily find the tune in a melodic dictionary if one had an idea of the correct spelling; the relatedness of tunes was a question of objective components. The tunes examined by Krohn, in contrast, exhibited a relatedness based on structural similarities, which suggested similar patterns of development and change. Such patterns were further interpreted in the light of genetic relatedness, and scholars soon labeled them with the appropriate term *tune families*. Krohn himself and his many successors refined and modified the genetic-historic approach to classification, and its underlying principles remain a part of many contemporary classificatory methodologies.

A third realm of classification has also been important to folk music study during the past century. This one has as its subject musical instruments. Unlike other areas of folk music classification, studies of instruments have often emphasized the comparative and universal more than the specific and the regional. Not surprisingly, the resulting methods reflect the disciplinary concerns of anthropology and systematic musicology (cf. Sachs 1929 and Schaeffner 1936). Even though evidence from specific cultures illustrates many organological theories, it also serves to justify claims for the universality of many instruments. Organologists have often aimed to conquer rather expansive theoretical turf, such as the evolution of instrument types throughout history (Sachs 1940). In general, approaches to the classification of instruments have been more lexicographic, although family-like groupings result also from the underlying evolutionary impetus.

The most widely accepted theory of instrumental ordering, published by Curt Sachs and Erich von Hornbostel in 1914, established four large groups of instruments on the basis of construction material and sounding mechanism: idiophones are "self-sounding" instruments (e.g., bells or xylophones); sound emanates from a stretched skin or other membrane in membranophones; strings are plucked, bowed, or struck to produce the sound from chordophones; and setting a column of air in vibration distinguishes aerophones (Hornbostel and Sachs 1961). The Sachs-Hornbostel method has encountered some criticism because of its imposition of hierarchical order (Lysloff and Matson 1985) and because nonacoustical (largely electronic) instruments do not lend themselves to classification in this manner, but the method remains the standard reference for most discussions of folk music instruments (e.g., the Diagram Group 1978).

While classification systems have focused primarily on the products of folk music, they have not completely ignored the processes, regarding them as links among the various products. Processes appear under three general categories: tune histories, tune families, and melodic change. Tune histories constitute the broadest category, but specific theories to describe the history of melodies are relatively undeveloped. The distinguishing feature of tune history as a category is what one might call the objective behavior of musical materials. Acceptance of such behavior is evident in studies of tunes that are diffused over vast cultural areas (e.g., Wiora 1953), sometimes with the implication that melodies or parts of tunes travel about more or less randomly and on their own volition (Tappert 1890). Such objectivity is relatively absent and unimportant in concepts of the tune family, and instead one finds explanations of how tune evolution takes place and why some versions appear and others do not. The genetic basis of the metaphorical family predetermines the extent and shape of representative melodic repertories. Melodic change, often a greater concern to ethnomusicologists studying folk music, may be less the product of an internal genetic cohesion than of contact with external musical and social forces. In general, however, many types of externally instigated change have not been primary interests in the development of classification systems. Some classifiers see radical change of this sort as a component of urban and modern influences, and therefore not related to the formation of folk music repertories; others regard external influences as disruptive of the order necessary for classification and therefore tantamount to a disintegration of the discursive boundaries of folk music (cf. Bartók 1931:53–80).

Classification: Concepts and Vocabulary

The initial step in most attempts to devise a classification system is determining which elements lend themselves to meaningful comparability and therefore identify the ways in which relatedness exists in the collections or repertories under examination. These elements range from very small units, some form of melodic morpheme, to large and abstract units, perhaps some type of tune gestalt (Suppan 1973 and Kuckertz 1963). The elements may be intrinsic to the structure of each piece or extrinsic to the piece and broadly characteristic of the larger repertory; an example of this sort of extrinsic element is mode or social function. Even these extrinsic factors tend to be measured by their influences on smaller elements, as in the complement and weighting of pitches in a particular piece that establish a relation with the modal possibilities of an entire repertory.

Smaller elements can be ordered in very precise ways, and for this reason lexicographic systems often concentrate initially on the smallest elements. The opening and final pitches of a piece, the initial interval, the relation between ambitus (the distance separating the highest and lowest notes) and central pitch all can be quantified, numerically or otherwise. Quantification allows one to establish an order, to spell out each melody and place it in a melodic lexicon near those melodies that have a similar spelling. The greater the number of small units that one quantifies, the more extensively the lexicographic system determines a place specific to individual melodies.

The next level often assumed by classification comprises the grammar and syntax of melody. This level moves from the strictly quantifiable and objective to the empirical and subjective. Thus, one not only identifies the elemental units but also formulates the basic patterns in which these units regularly occur. It is theoretically possible to interpret the patterns formed at this level for lexicographic purposes, but most classifiers concerned with aspects of grammatical and syntactical patterns also investigate them to determine the bases for tune families or histories. Genre is first evident at this level, in some cases in only general characteristics but in others through fairly specific structures and processes of change. Whereas ballad and epic require more extensive narrative structures, lyric folk songs and the blues may allow essential flexibility at this level. In studies of lyric folk song, Judith McCulloh has suggested that examining the function of the "smallest rearrangeable unit of text" provides the key to establishing the level at which understanding and exploration of the genre can take place (1970:7). These units appear throughout repertories of lyric song and in essence define the repertories by the particular clusters that they form (McCulloh 1983:42).

The establishment of criteria for using melodic contour for classification has been one of the more persistent ways of de-emphasizing the role of smaller elements while bringing light to bear on the overall form of melody. The earliest advocate of classifying primarily on the basis of contour was Sirvart Poladian, who aimed to find some means of extending methods that worked well for specific repertories to a larger, more comparative framework. The salient features of contour were those that had widespread distribution in a large number of very different repertories—for example, descent to the final note, which

Poladian held to be "one musical feature [that] seems common to most folk songs" (1942:207). Perhaps most important to Poladian was his belief that contour was one of the few melodic factors that song variants did not alter, thus making it an extremely stable representation of any repertory or style (ibid.:210–11). More recently, George List has made similar claims for the salience of melodic aspects abstracted by contour, again noting that melodic contour may provide one of the most effective keys for determining the existence and limits of universality in folk music (List 1978 and 1985; see also Mosely 1964:11–12).

Few areas of classification have weathered the storms of criticism as indomitably as modes. The application of modal theories often takes the form of esoteric studies directed to a small fraternity of cognoscenti. That may be the stimulus of or response to the polemical debate that modal theories sometimes spur, but rarely do modal theories seem designed for broader appeal or the methodological corollary that lexicographic ordering permits. In several cases, debates over the role of modes in folk music take on a life of their own, abandoning empirical studies of standard collections and the new evidence that fieldwork would impart (cf. Cazden 1971 and Bronson 1972). In Anglo-American ballad scholarship, polemic was a part of modal research from virtually the moment it appeared. In the first edition of his *English Folk Song: Some Conclusions* in 1907, Cecil Sharp included a chapter on modes (pages 36–53), in which he claimed that the melodic material of English folk song was essentially related to the diatonic modes of the medieval Latin church. His aim was twofold. On one hand, this connection with an earlier stratum of European musical life overlaid folk song with the patina of age, concomitantly distancing it from popular, urban music employing major and minor modality. On the other hand, Sharp hoped that folk song would be a new font for the English composer, hardly an unusual desire in an age of nationalism but one that would benefit markedly from a demonstration of the theoretically sound structure of folk music. Sharp's rather prescribed goals notwithstanding, many successors took up the modal banner, insisting that Anglo-American folk songs were rooted in intricate and occasionally fantastic designs for the interrelation of the church modes. Bertrand H. Bronson conceived of this pattern as a seven-pointed star, with each mode forming one point and mixed modes located elsewhere about the star (1969:85).

The persistence of modal debates has done little to clarify problems of classification and has instead occluded the potential for establishing more accessible criteria for relatedness. That this persistence continues to petrify some of the most sacred of canonic formulae, including those encasing the Child ballads, cannot be denied. But mode has not always worked to the detriment of classification. Its role in many non-Western musical systems is undeniable, and we base our systematic understanding of such musical cultures as those of Iran, the Arabic Middle East, and the Indian subcontinent on elaborate modal frameworks. Several European scholars were more judicious in their claims for modes; Bartók, for example, used mode as one criterion for the age of a folk song, thus employing mode to corroborate, rather than set, the discursive boundaries of Hungarian folk music.

For a system of classification to offer significant insight into the organization of folk music repertories and style it must ideally combine the various levels and foci that this section has surveyed. One of the most masterful syntheses of diverse approaches is that which Béla Bartók, in collaboration with Zoltán Kodály, applied to Eastern European folk music, with especially valuable results in the examination of Hungarian collections (Bartók 1931, Kodály 1960, Erdely 1965:43–73, and Herzog 1937:54). Bartók combined lexicographic methods developed by Finnish scholars with classificatory criteria that would identify both genetic and historical patterns. He began by simply counting the number of lines in a melody. Next, the intervallic distance of the final note of each line from the finalis of the song was measured. The number of syllables in each line

Mikor a nagy erdön kimész

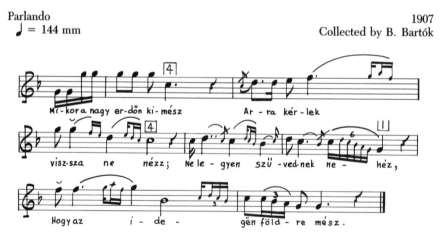

Parlando
♩ = 144 mm

1907
Collected by B. Bartók

Translation

Would you get out of the big forest,
Look not behind you,
Lest your heart be heavy
When you set foot in a foreign land.

EXAMPLE 3
(cf. Bartók 1931:7, 107, and Section A1, p. 6)

was then represented, and finally the ambitus of the song was stated as two numerals, one the lowest note of the melody and the other the highest. A string of numbers, then, appeared as an abstract lexicographic representation of the melody. Bartók's method may be illustrated with the folk song "Mikor a nagy erdön kimész" (example 3). The figures Bartók used to designate this song are 4̲ 4̲ ⊔, 8, 1–8. These figures mean that the song is a four-line tune whose first and second lines end on ♭♯, and whose third line ends on ♭♯. All lines consist of eight syllables, the lowest note being ♭♯, and the highest ♭♯ (Bartók 1931:7).

Bartók's classification system offers other descriptive insights, most importantly those linking style to age (cf. Kodály 1960:23–68). When a piece has a restricted ambitus or lines with a small number of syllables, it comes from an older stratum of the repertory (Bartók 1931:8–9). Rhythmic and metric considerations are also significant determinants of age and style. The Old Style Hungarian melodies had a free, speech-like rhythm that Bartók calls *parlando rubato*. In contrast, a *tempo giusto* style, characterized by a more regularized, dance-derived rhythm, predominates in the New Style (ibid.:9). Bartók's method is remarkably thorough, and it elucidates many intricacies of style and structure in Hungarian folk music. It is less successful in its explanation of non-Hungarian repertories, where, for example, syllable count in each line plays a less significant role than in Hungarian folk music. The system founders when applied to non-Western music. The criteria of his system required that Bartók claim Arabic folk music to be at an incipient evolutionary stage because of the prevalence of short lines and single melodic motifs (Bartók 1920:489), whereas variable line lengths and the appearance of simple and complex melodic motifs together are widespread in all genres of Arabic music. Bartók's approach to classification was, therefore, most effective when applied to the repertories that he knew best, whose idiosyncracies he understood most intimately; that the approach did not succeed in becoming universal is hardly exceptional in the history of folk music classification.

A wide range of regional and ethnic criteria has produced many approaches to classification. The boundaries that such criteria demarcate are, of course, geographic and social, and therefore one recognizes the considerable potential for determining some aspects of universal ordering. A frequent qualification of indigenous classification is the association of certain pieces with the place in which one lives and the understanding that certain other pieces come from elsewhere. The venue for the pieces from elsewhere may vary; it may be another region or another social setting—an urban center, for example, in contradistinction to a rural area. Folk taxonomies in northeastern Iran and Afghanistan almost always stress this contrast between rural and urban, even when the real sources of the folk music repertories are more complex and mixed (cf. Blum

1974:86 and Sakata 1983:53–63). Folk musicians who perform throughout an ethnically pluralistic area often rely on a complex indigenous classification system to indicate which repertories are appropriate for the audiences in different parts of the area (cf. Blum 1972 and Bohlman 1980). Regional and ethnic criteria often classify repertories in a fairly loose fashion. The criteria with which Vance Randolph ordered his large collections of Ozark folk songs do not transfer as a cohesive group to other repertories, for despite his use of some general categories (e.g., "British ballads and songs," in Randolph 1980, vol. 1) he also uses more specific regional categories (e.g., "Songs of the South and West," in ibid., vol. 2). The larger classification system itself only applies to the Ozarks, whereas the individual parts might describe other areas of the United States.

The most ambitious attempt to forge a classification system by combining regional and ethnic criteria with social and functional aspects of music has been Alan Lomax's cantometrics project (Lomax 1968 and 1976). Cantometrics posits that social structure is the model for musical performance and sound and that repertories form on the basis of unified expression of social structure. In a sense, this idea is an extension of the culture-area *(Kulturkreis)* concept so important to comparative musicology. But in this concept, history and diffusion of cultural traits determine large areas, whereas in cantometrics cultural boundaries form from within the culture—they are buttressed by the uses and functions of culture. Most important to the classificatory potential of cantometrics is the assertion by its advocates that the relation between social structure and musical expression is quantifiable: thirty-seven criteria of musical production can be measured easily and compared accurately using computers (figure 2). In addition, a detailed map reveals classification according to six world regions, fifty-six culture areas, and 233 specific cultures. The difficulties of precise comparability notwithstanding, cantometrics is not unlike many other classification systems in that it begins by attempting to identify the appropriate levels of comparison and then examines them in diverse settings to establish criteria that universalize the structure of music's discursive boundaries. And, like other systems with an agenda of universality, cantometrics has encountered the persistence of differentiation within those boundaries, thus limiting comparability to the specific and requiring modification of the classificatory criteria when cantometrics approaches the universal.

The Dialectical Concerns of Classification

Accessibility to the general and differentiation of the specific: ideally, all classification systems must achieve both. The classifier must discern how each piece is like the others in a given repertory while maintaining the integrity of

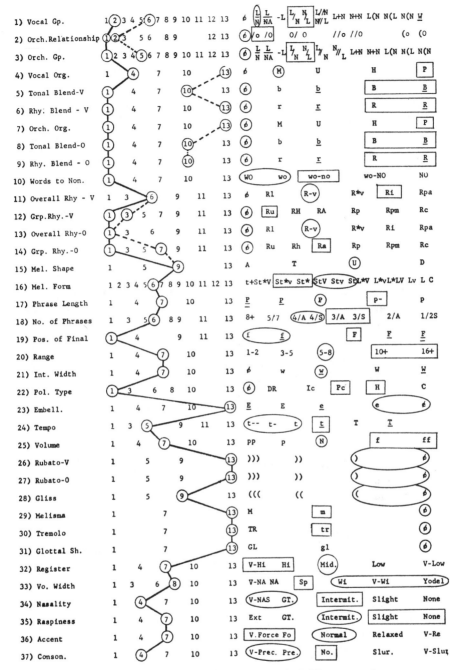

FIGURE 2. Cantometrics profile for Europe. The solid line traces the course of the main type of European song—solo, unaccompanied performance of foursquare strophes in simple meter. The dashed line shows a second type—simple group organization in polyphony with good tonal blend. This profile most strongly resembles Old High Culture. (Source: Lomax 1968:100. Reprinted by permission of the author.)

the piece by recognizing its differences. Classification is, at its best, a dynamic process that allows for the changeability of folk music and its repertories and for influences from diverse sources. On the surface, classification may seem to seek ways of closing a repertory, but underneath it must be flexible enough to respond to the dynamic forces that constantly reshape folk music aesthetically and functionally. Classification must confront and explain both the products and the processes of folk music in a dialectical way if it is to be as broadly effective and meaningful as possible.

Description and prescription. Descriptive approaches seek to define repertories in relation to elements that are stable and structurally fundamental over time. Description is inductive in the sense that it observes the specific first and then devises the appropriate classification system on that basis. Theoretically, the potential for true universality is greater with descriptive approaches, but practically, the census of characteristics consistently observed over sufficiently long periods can never be quite complete enough. Prescription, in contrast, allows the making of choices on the basis of limited examples that permit the extrapolation of an idealized repertory and the classification thereof. The classifier may prescribe those levels that he or she believes salient to comparability and then define the canon accordingly. The expansion of field collections may or may not justify the canon, but this may not be important to the relevance of classification, for prescription accepts that certain patterns of relatedness are ideals, or abstractions of a census too unwieldy to represent in all its details. The combination of description and prescription depends on the repertory or collection that the scholar aims to classify and on the role fieldwork will play in continuing to expand the collection; it also depends on the relative needs for lexicographic access or stylistic analysis.

Emic and etic. By referring to emic and etic approaches as dialectics I do not mean to pair folk with outsider classification. Rather, I wish to suggest two philosophical goals that underlie many approaches to classification. One extreme argues that true classification of a repertory lies in the collective unconscious of the community sharing that repertory; the other extreme believes that there are objective rules of structure and form over which the folk exert no control. Those approaches that attempt to reflect emic classification demonstrate great variety. Some aim to elucidate an extensive epistemological understanding of the way music is expressive in different cultures; Steven Feld's studies of the Kaluli of Papua New Guinea, for example, have revealed a complex representation of the culture's avian-derived mythological concepts in its attitudes toward and performance of music (1982). Other emic approaches rely on a deeper historical understanding of a society's classification of folk music; Stephen Blum, for example, has shown that the attitudes toward folk music in northeastern Iran (Khorasan) are related in complex ways to the long interaction of oral and written genres of music and poetry (1974). To some extent, all classification systems reflect the etic motivations of their designers. When etic motivations bear little or no resemblance to emic concepts, a classification system may result that has little historical validity. The efforts of Cecil Sharp, Olive Dame Campbell, and others to impose on many Appalachian communities folk music repertories replete with Child ballads and morris dances is one of the most glaring examples of the disjunction between emic and etic concepts of classification (cf. Whisnant 1983, esp. 105–79).

Aesthetic-formal and cultural-functional. Aesthetic and formal criteria have been fundamental to most genetic-historical classificatory schemes. Form and structure provide the basic vocabulary for lexicographic ordering and for the relatedness of pieces and genres one to another. In some cases, such approaches only prescribe the aesthetic realm of a single repertory; they may also elucidate the structural elements that make the formation of repertories possible, thereby extending their application to a more general level. Reliance on the role of social function in shaping repertories often produces a somewhat different way of ordering. In extreme cases, functional criteria completely replace formal relatedness. Many of the most effective approaches, including the approach developed by Bartók and Kodály, combine aesthetic and formal considerations with the cultural and functional, thus explaining a vast array of differentiated elements with a single classification system.

Similarity and difference. The measurement of similarity and difference is central to many approaches to classification (Nettl 1983:118–19). Does one classify on the basis of similarity? Or are differences more relevant to the boundaries that a particular repertory exhibits? These questions raise even larger ones. Is a classification system determined by internal coherence? Or, rather, does order accrue as a result of contrast with external genres and repertories? Clearly, the answers to these questions differ from repertory to repertory. In some cases, similarity may be so widespread that it loses all meaning as a criterion for classification, and the classifier must turn to the ways in which differences appear. Extreme difference, in contrast, might belie the true sense of coherence that determines a repertory, perhaps because of even greater difference when compared to other repertories. Choices to emphasize the role of similarity or difference often reflect the balance between descriptive and prescriptive approaches that a classification system illustrates.

Diachronic and synchronic. When musical change serves as a measurement of the differentiation that folk music repertories exhibit, classification necessarily includes many diachronic considerations. The historical component of genetic-historical approaches is essentially diachronic. In the methods of Bartók and Kodály, diachronic evidence and results predominate; Nettl, too, has argued persuasively for the historical motive that pervades many approaches to understanding folk music (e.g., 1973:10–11). When stylistic and structural reasons seem to underlie the variation that appears in folk music repertories, synchronic analysis may prove more useful. We may find, for example, that there is a wide and relatively sparse distribution of tune or text types, regardless of the general patterns of diachronic change. Modal classification, too, relies relatively little on diachronic change, though the work of Harold Powers is an important exception (e.g., 1970). The more internal melodic elements are denominated as abstract entities, the more synchronic differences play a role in classification.

The specific and the universal. This dialectic is one of the most problematic in all classification endeavors. The classifier faces the paradox of refining the system for one repertory so precisely that it no longer has general applications or of accounting for the general characteristics of many repertories so broadly that no single repertory really fits very well. This paradox is seldom lost upon scholars who devote themselves to classification, for most demonstrate an awareness of the need to arrive at a synthesis of the two extremes (e.g., Poladian 1942 and Väisänen 1949). The most successful syntheses occur at a more moderate level, when one generally acceptable system is adapted to several other repertories. Bartók, for example, refined the Finnish genetic-historical method so that it would classify Hungarian folk music and other regional repertories of Eastern Europe. In most cases, his refinements offered new insight into the structure and history of Eastern European repertories. The same methods applied to such non-Western repertories as Turkish and Arabic rural musical styles produced spurious results. In short, Bartók significantly expanded the specificity of the Finnish method but was unable to render the method universal. The classificatory dialectic of particular versus universal underscores a fundamental question in folk music scholarship: is folk music really a universal genre of expressive behavior? If so, must its particular manifestations—its local and regional repertories and forms of musical behavior—be comparable on a universal scale? Even the most effective classification systems fail to provide firm answers to such questions, but they do serve to remind us that every repertory of folk music contains elements of both the particular and the universal.

Folk Music and Art Music:
Classification and the Composer

Although many of the classificatory concepts devised by folk music scholarship are primarily concerned with the interrelations of various folk music repertories, the urge to understand through classification has also guided much of the thinking about the ways in which folk music interacts with other genres, especially with "composed" art music. I emphasize the action of composing art music because this action identifies a significant aspect of this type of classification, whose end result is usually less a matter of inventory or schematic representation than of use; it is thus a restating of perceived meaning in folk music within a new musical context. Composers in many musical cultures turn to folk music in search of new meanings—or, more precisely, special meanings—and thereby advocate a personal understanding of the broader cultural role folk music stands to play: crystallizing nationalism, encapsulating the essence of musical style and structure, or serving as a font for expanding the musical vocabulary. The composer often bases his or her use of folk music in an art music context on classificatory decisions, and it is not uncommon to find the composer engaged in other aspects of classification in relation to or in preparation for the resituating of folk music in the art music context. Bartók and Vaughan Williams are but two of the twentieth-century composers whose collection and investigation of folk music were inseparable from their creative philosophy. In the history of Western art music, the motivations for using folk music have been many, but they have rarely been completely absent during the formation and change of a musical style (Wiora 1957).

Folk music appears in art music in two ways, each demonstrating many variations. In the first of these, the integrity of the piece of folk music remains. One can easily recognize the tune or another musical parameter that the composer attempts to represent with some degree of literalness. For Bartók the folk melody used in this way was "like a gem in its setting" (1972b:169). In contrast, the composer may seek not to maintain the external integrity of a piece of folk music but rather to penetrate to the essence of folk song style and to appropriate this essence for the composition of art music. The composer may have very specific designs for folk music used in this way. Bartók, for example, wrote works in Bulgarian rhythms that did not contain direct settings of Bulgarian folk dances. Other composers may think of folk-like styles with more stereotypical goals in mind, as in writing in the style of a musette with a sustained drone and narrow melodic ambitus standing in for a more thorough consideration of the complexities of bagpipe playing.

To portray the history of the interrelation of folk and art music as a commonplace activity of composers can easily oversimplify the more pervasive relationship between different genres of music that characterizes most musical cultures. One must exercise considerable caution when discussing the composer as the primary creative agent in the processes of exchange and cross-influence. The folk music specialist is often neither less adept nor less willing to exercise creativity by turning to numerous musical repertories for new sources. And unquestionably, religious and popular music genres draw from folk music, which in turn accepts influences from those genres. In short, the relationship between folk music and art music is not an isolated phenomenon based only on the decisions of a few musicians but is one expression of the complex patterns of change that continually shape different genres in all musical cultures (Ward 1986). It is an interrelation marked by dynamism and multidimensionality, which are among the most important markers of folk music in the modern world.

Folk music scholarship has not always accepted the multidimensionality of this interrelation. The theory of *gesunkenes Kulturgut* established primacy for art music, which yielded pieces to folk repertories through a process of "sinking" or deteriorating to meet the prerequisites of survival in oral tradition (Naumann 1922). The first articulation of theories accounting for individual creation of folk music also saw as fairly unidirectional the movement from folk music. John Meier's motto for folk music resulting from this process was *Kunstlieder im Volksmund* (art songs in the voice of the folk). As far-reaching as Meier's claims were in the first decades of the twentieth century, they recognized creativity in only one of the musical genres he sought to pair. Hungarian concepts of classification discern historical patterns within the movement among genres, portraying the interrelation of folk and art music as different potential lineages. One lineage yielded the folk-like art songs *(volkstümliche Kunstlieder)* of nine-teenth-century Hungarian urban genres, which benefited from the influx to the city of rural Hungarians—the practitioners of folk music (Bartók 1972b:164). A rather different and more direct history is possible when composers of art music penetrate folk music to determine its essence and then to use this essence in art music. Only certain results are possible from this process, giving it a somewhat limited dimensionality. Bartók, for example, could accept the pos-sibility of molding only a tonal musical style on folk music. "Folk music [is] always tonal, and an atonal folk music [is] totally unimaginable. One could therefore not base an atonal twelve-tone music on tonal folk music" (ibid.:174).

If we place the composer of art music in the role of classifier, it is hardly surprising that each has specific goals for his treatment of folk music. Again, the classifier has fewer universal than particular criteria for interpreting folk music. The ultimate result of using folk music for particular ends is stabilizing an individual style and sustaining its mediation of a canon. The abundance of literature devoted to Beethoven's use of folk music, for example, largely shows how folk music came to shape his style. Folk music did not leave a deep impression of an especially Austrian folk melos, and in fact Beethoven ranged throughout the folk repertories of Europe in search of sources for the more than two hundred examples of folk melodies that scholars have identified in Beethoven's oeuvre (Braun 1982–83:287). Bartók, too, did not limit himself to Hungarian folk music of the Old Style when composing. Despite the remarkable diversity in his personal style, it is very distinct from the many folk music styles that inspired him.

What are some of the qualities composers identify in folk music when drawing upon it as a source? One of the most common is the symbolism of the rural, as in the designation of a symphony movement as "pastorale." Evoking this symbolism can involve explicit or implicit musical references; one may use folk music itself as a source or create a style that is folk-like. For some composers and scholars, the meaning of folk music for classical styles is much more profound than an evocative symbolism. Walter Wiora argues for a stylistic unity that pervades all German song but begins, nevertheless, with folk song. The nationalistic overtones and linguistic biases of such an argument are, of course, obvious, yet there can be no doubt that Wiora's scheme for classifying the forms and history of German song are predicated on a sound understanding of the genre and a vast pool of examples (Wiora 1971b). The search for *Ur*-forms in folk music further identifies quite precisely the musical traits that distinguish the genre. Vaughan Williams, for example, transferred his belief in the modal moorings of English folk song to his own compositional style. Whereas many composers concerned themselves primarily with the melodic purity of some folk music, Bartók saw it as the basis for harmonic complexity, speculating that the simpler a melody was, the more individual its harmonization could be (Bartók 1972b:170). As much as we might feel that Bartók is demonstrating homage to folk music, we must also wonder to what degree he is compelled to transpose the belief in vertical complexity so characteristic of Western art music to folk music. When he states that the simplicity of "Arabic peasant music" lends itself to many harmonic possibilities (ibid.), it seems likely that his concept of classification derives more from art music than from the folk music it seeks to interpret.

The interrelation of folk and art music forms yet another classificatory dialectic, one that more often than not has slightly discomfiting ramifications because of the implicitly negative value judgments that too often appear in contrastive phrases like "high versus low culture." But the dialectic also bears witness to some positive conclusions that contribute considerably to the study of folk music. First, the composer turns to folk music because of its creative potential; in the composer's treatment the folk melody is not a frozen artifact whose survival in oral tradition depends on immutably simple structures. Second, the engagement of art musicians with folk music reveals even more clearly the fallacy of constructing any classification system based on stratified models of noninteracting genres; folk and art music are rarely not influencing each other in some way. Finally, the dialectical interrelation of folk and art music is remarkably dynamic and multidimensional, revealing complex processes of change that occur as much in folk music as they do in art music. It is hardly surprising, then, that this dialectic, too, has failed to produce a single, universal method of classification.

Classification and Defining (Defending) the Canon

Few successful classification schemes can avoid paring away some extraneous material from the repertories they order. If nothing else, classification must be manageable; it must extract from the amorphous whole some basic musical structures, whether these are abstract melodic types or simply common and persistent tunes. But the process of paring away is fraught with problems. The distinction between decisions that include or exclude is often difficult to make. A reductionist momentum may also build up, resulting in eventual claims that only a few tunes or texts truly represent a repertory; some of the otherwise fine attempts to classify the Anglo-American folk music repertory have suffered this fate (cf. Bayard 1950, esp. 3–4). Bartók, too, was far more comfortable with the exclusiveness of the Old Style and New Style, which were relatively purged of foreign, urban, and popular influences, than with the Mixed Style, which bore witness to the changes through which modern Hungarian folk music had passed.

The extreme form of the penetration of classification to the specific is the gradual replacement of observed and collected tradition with the system that has purported to define it. In other words, the classification system becomes the surrogate for the tradition itself. The emergence of a surrogate tradition is the most extreme and insidious product of canon-formation. The initial assertions that English ballads and dance genres were the archetypes of folk music in the Appalachians quickly became a surrogate tradition, spurring collectors to discover songs that would justify the appropriate classification systems, especially the system devised by Child. As a result, many of the same collectors ignored the more popular black-influenced styles that were flourishing in the same region. Under Nazism in Germany during the 1930s and early 1940s, folk music classification declared a sort of independence from ethnography, thus allowing the establishment of claims that Germanic and Nordic folk music was somehow central to European folk music in general (cf. Danckert 1987:21–26).

Classification is almost never the product of strictly objective goals. Whatever the claims for discerning a repertory's "internal order" may be, value judgments inevitably attend the choice of criteria for comparability and, more pregnant as a force molding the ordering decisions, those pieces that actually constitute the repertory abstracted by classification. More often than not, those who most effectively use classification in this way are no longer aware of their redefinition of tradition. "The main danger in classification," warned George Herzog, "is that it leads to assuming that objects in a storeroom were originally created and deposited in that order" (1937:51). The value judgments of classifiers may initially be very personal and idiosyncratic, but the discursive boundaries they set may assume a rigidity that renders them a surrogate of the tradition itself. Once a means of defining the canon, these discursive boundaries serve only to defend it.

Classification constantly concerns itself with the discursive boundaries—internal and external—of folk music. Whenever one talks about folk music in a systematic way, one engages in some form of classification. Our theoretical vocabulary is full of designations that accept or reject, acknowledge or ignore certain approaches to classification. Performers engage in a form of classification when they choose a particular means of interacting with different communities. The mass mediation of folk music, too, relies on widespread understanding of certain levels of classification. These various ways of discussing and portraying the interrelatedness of folk music may define it as a genre in restrictive or expansive terms. At some levels, the discourse of classification therefore serves only to perpetuate old canons; at others, it forges new canons.

FOUR

The Social Basis of Folk Music: A Sense of Community, a Sense of Place

[Poesy] lived in the ear of the people, issuing forth from the lips and harps of the living singers: it sang of history, events, mysteries, wonders, and omens: it was the blossom of the unique character of a people, its language, and its land, its occupation and biases, its suffering and arrogance, its music and soul.

Johann Gottfried Herder (1975:167)

The first function of music, especially of folk music, is to produce a feeling of security for the listener by voicing the particular quality of a land and the life of its people.

Alan Lomax (1960:xv)

Traditional music, ethnic music, popular music, people's music, working-class music, national music, regional music, *chanson populaire, Volkslied, Volks-gesang:* the myriad terms used in various contexts to designate the genre of expressive behavior this book more generally calls folk music reflect a wide range of concepts, methodologies, and ideologies. Whatever the differences such terms suggest, they share a common tendency to identify groups of individuals: the folk, the people, the nation. Coupled with more specific qualifiers, the terms further identify which group, which traditional culture, shares a body of music, even how that music has come to symbolize the group: Jewish traditional music, German student songs, New England sea chanteys. Folk music bears witness to both implicit and explicit social bases.

The various rubrics applied to folk music have derived from two fundamental considerations of social organization. The first emphasized the primacy of the group or community itself; the second laid greater emphasis on the role of place, whether geographically, politically, or culturally situated (Bauman 1972:32–33). These two considerations differ according to the relative weight they assign to internal and external processes of cultural production. When group or community is seen as the source of social organization, folk music originates internally and is shaped by the needs and practices of the group; when a concept of place predominates, folk music responds to such external developments, as the intensification of nationalism and the influence of musical genres not specific to the group. More recently, several approaches stress a fuller realization of the shaping role that performance and contact with other cultures play in determining the social basis of folklore (ibid.:passim). The result of these more performance-directed approaches has been to modify the frequent overreliance on coherent group or prescribed geography, thereby accounting more broadly for the processes of change and a multiplicity of influences. But the attention to groups as conglomerates of individuals who share some aspects of culture and are linked in some way by folklore does not diminish when performance models are applied. The social basis, too, remains essential to the understanding of folk music as the product of changing boundaries and shifting group membership.

Because folk music is inevitably a performed genre, it is essential to consider its social basis. Who performs? To whom are performances directed? Is folk music shared broadly throughout a community? Or is it maintained by a small group of specialists? The answers to these questions differ significantly from culture to culture, indicating further the vastly different social bases that folk music may exhibit. As a performed genre, folk music can live in a community only through repetition or re-creation, both of which characteristically require performer and audience. Folk music is therefore distinct from folklore genres that can survive as artifacts, which may or may not assume new life depending on their relation to a community's social basis over time. In short, folk music requires a vital social basis for its continued practice.

The close interrelation of folk music and its social basis has been central to many theories of folk music. In some of these theories, folk music and social structure are inseparable; they mirror each other. In other theories, the complexity of musical activity symbolizes only certain aspects of a group's social basis—the direction of change, for example, or the measurement of external influences. The present chapter surveys a range of theoretical approaches that explore folk music's role in culture. Because of the complexity of this role—for example, the prerequisite of performance and the frequency of specialization—closer scrutiny of folk music stands to yield considerable understanding of the social basis of folklore, especially for those modern societies in which the canons of folk music are constantly changing.

Social Basis Spawned at the Cultural Core

The earliest European theories articulating an interrelation of folk music and social basis portrayed folk music as if it were the cultural core of noncomplex society. Speculations on the nature of folk music and the social organization of nature were tautologically circumscribed (Herder 1975:167–85). Protoevolutionary models portrayed music and the other arts as immanent in culture; these arts in turn owed their cultural basis to the link between humans and nature (e.g., Forkel 1788:69). To understand music was to understand the social basis for human expression. Folk music was the crystallization of the cultural core. As folk music was structured, so too was the rest of society.

The location of folk music at the cultural core has persisted to the present day, even though the reasons and motivations for insisting on such location have proceeded along different paths and contrast greatly. Both Enlightenment and early Romantic writers often portrayed folk music as a bridge between the natural and the civilized worlds. Both humans and animals naturally produced song, but for the former there were also an inherent order and the ability to express emotion. For Herder and subsequent generations of writers on folk music, it was the language of the soul or the heart (Forkel ibid.); folk music encapsulated the cultural core before society complicated it.

Nineteenth-century Europe came to accept and insist upon more complex models of society. The nation more fully resembled society in its ultimate form, and nationalism epitomized the cultural core. Burgeoning nationalism was nothing short of a primary impetus to the development of full-blown theories of folk music. It is hardly surprising, then, that folk music quickly came to symbolize another cultural core, that of the nation. If the Enlightenment model of folk music applied to all human society, the nineteenth-century model had geographic and political boundaries. Folk music found a place on the map.

In addition to the nationalist ends that motivated much European folk music research, other concepts lent it leitmotifs suggesting a powerful sense of place. Of these, the persistent urban-rural dichotomy is best known. This dichotomy did not simply derive from two contrasting social structures but was often invested with a real recognition of physical distance. Bartók claimed that it was essential to collect folk music in villages "as far as possible from the centers of civilization and transportation routes" (Bartók 1972a:159). Conversely, the city has more recently become the focus of intensive folk music research because it is a center for the convergence of different folk music styles and repertories

(Nettl 1976:123–36). Even the folk music revival of the 1950s and early 1960s is often delimited by the additional adjective *urban*.

For reasons both political and historical, regionalism has supplanted many folk music concepts earlier shaped by nationalism. No American region has benefited more from the practice of equating a body of folk music with a prescribed area than the South (Malone 1979, esp. 4–17). Linking all explanations for the implicit stylistic unity of Southern folk music is a list of factors yielding stability. And if there is a region of the United States whose very geography is a source of stability, then, say the advocates of a Southern regional style, it is the South. Southern folk music, Alan Lomax says,

> is an antique tradition with traits from many parts of Britain, moulded into a distinctive regional style by a common pattern of life. . . . Poverty and isolation permitted this backwoods music to develop on its own for more than a century. Thus it grew strong enough to absorb urban influences and produce a regional style (hillbilly) which has attracted vast city audiences (Lomax 1960:153; the parentheses are Lomax's).

Another means of defining folk music's position at the cultural core has been the search for a stylistic essence or unity that realizes the infrastructure of society. Unlike geographically determined models, the stylistic approach conceives of a cultural core that characterizes the human composition of a community rather than its physical location. The descriptions of culture that result from the stylistic approach sometimes appear little different from those that a geographic approach would have produced. In fact, several of the most influential stylistic approaches continue to employ metaphors to describe the relation of musical style to location.

The most influential conceptualization of geography's impact on culture to inform European, especially German, folk music research was *Kulturkreislehre* (theory of culture area). Initially growing from German theories of cultural history and ethnology, *Kulturkreislehre* was refashioned by musicologists to determine patterns of stylistic integrity that would make comparison possible. Implicit in this notion of comparison was the possibility that musical style could develop in specific, rather than random, patterns that would allow the music of one culture to demonstrate palpable similarities, even parallels, when compared to music of another culture (Schneider 1976:10). The greater the similarity in the course of cultural history, the more extensive the stylistic similarity of folk music. Werner Danckert (e.g., 1937), a proponent of *Kulturkreislehre*, perceived remarkable degrees of unity in the folk music styles of large cultural regions, especially in Europe, the focus of Danckert's primary research. Common historical origins enabled musical traits to migrate from nation to nation within Europe, further strengthening the stylistic unity that stretched from the "primitive" to the "high cultures" of the Continent (Danckert 1970:3). The folk music of Europe produced a closed "style-province," justified by the singular direction of its cultural history (ibid.:4).

The most extreme position of folk music style as cultural core has been staked out by Lomax in his sweeping theory of cantometrics. The basis of cantometrics is the claim that many aspects of society imprint themselves in music because music is ipso facto a communal activity. Singing "invites group participation. Whether chorally performed or not, however, the chief function of song is to express the shared feelings and mold the joint activities of some human community" (Lomax 1968:3). If at first glance Lomax's statements have the ring of platitudes, his plans for quantifying the stylistic role of music at the cultural core soon specify and focus the claims of cantometrics. A unified cultural core, signified by the degree of collectivity, is more musical than one that is not unified; extensive and shared musicality result when a society normally acts in concert.

> Those areas that seem "most musical" in the popular estimation—Central Europe, Africa, and Polynesia—are also renowned for their highly coordinated group singing and dancing. In other words, Africans, Polynesians, and Central Europeans are seen as having an extraordinary talent for music, precisely because they are adepts at cohesive kinesthetic behavior (Lomax 1968:171).

Both *Kulturkreislehre* and cantometrics falter when musical style fails to exhibit normative patterns throughout a given society. Attractive because of their virtually one-to-one equation of musical style and cultural core, the theories often account poorly for societies in which such an equation does not exist. This is especially true of societies in which change—social and musical—has not been unidirectional, as Danckert perceived it in Europe, or where contact at a distance from the cultural core has fragmented musical style. If, indeed, there are societies in which music does not simply function "to augment the solidarity of a group" (ibid.), folk music style may have no more than a tangential relation to the shifting characteristics of the cultural core.

The equation of musical style and cultural core often results in the extension of ideological overtones to folk music. If music stands in such close relation to society, it clearly exhibits considerable power. Few attribute a broader range of power to music than Jacques Attali: "It is an attribute of power in all its forms" (1985:6). In his mystical rendition of Marxism, Attali quantifies and qualifies the equation of music and cultural core, seemingly transmogrifying the equation to the function of ritual, whereby music not only replicates but generates social structure: "Music creates political order because it is a minor form of sacrifice" (ibid.:25). Such power is rarely lost upon those who would envision a canon of folk music with a specifically ideological resonance for society (Wong 1984). This ideological function is undoubtedly one of the primary motivating forces for the formation of new canons of folk music.

Religious doctrine, too, has often recognized the power of music to bolster the cultural core. In some cases, as in Judaism, the line between traditional music and the music of tradition has been nebulous for centuries. Religious subgenres of folk music occupy considerable portions of the total corpus of folk music in some parts of Scandinavia, especially in Norway. In many areas of German settlement in the American Midwest, hymns and other religious genres passed from written sources to oral tradition within several generations, thereafter constituting the largest body of folk music for many German-American communities (Bohlman 1984b; for a different ethnic group, see Frey 1960). Just as the exigencies of immigration necessarily reshaped the cultural core in the case of these German-American communities, so too did music undergo considerable change in order to retain its close proximity to the core. Thus the equation of folk music and cultural core does not require the stasis or immutability of the core. But as change does occur, it becomes evident that external influences also come to bear on folk music's social basis: influences emanating from the cultural boundaries.

The Social Basis Emanating from the Boundaries

As modernization has deflected much of the centripetal attraction that justified the equation of musical style with cultural core, folk music research has increasingly focused on diverse influences. Theories that large geographic units like nations or continents were composed of smaller units like regions or pristine rural villages have become less and less tenable during the twentieth century as the borders of these units were battered by war and their populations often took up residence elsewhere. Old cultural cores wore down and new communities arose; contact with the external world became a physical reality, which in turn made cultural boundaries and differences more visible. Folk music has not, however, diminished in its symbolic role of distilling and representing a community's social basis; rather, it has responded to a changing social basis by changing itself, absorbing different repertoires, and reflecting a stylistic congeries.

Cultural boundaries are not themselves a product of modernization; the relative ability of such boundaries to include or exclude, to sanction or thwart change, however, has become a more significant determinant of community in the twentieth century. In settings where cultural contact is pervasive, the assertion of cultural boundaries is often a matter of choice, making them flexible

(Barth 1969:14); elsewhere, observance of boundaries may be a product of normative social exchange (Lockwood 1984:221). The formation of ethnic boundaries in the American immigrant setting, therefore, accompanies a growing awareness of folk music styles other than those previously situated at the cultural core. Technology, too, breaches the boundaries of musical repertories and styles, for the mass media make contact with music cultures throughout the world a common occurrence.

It is now generally accepted that ubiquitous culture contact has not caused the wholesale disappearance of cultural distinctiveness or the use of folk music to signify that distinctiveness. Contemporary theory asserts that the identity that shapes groups and generates folklore may be both shared and differential, that is, derived from both core and boundary, similarities and differences (Bauman 1972:34). Such theory goes a long way to explain the complexity of ethnic groups in industrialized nations. When we go so far as to say "the term 'folk' can refer to any group of people whatsoever who share at least one common factor" (Dundes 1965:2), we tender great latitude to the social basis of folklore. But does an equivalent latitude also extend to repertories of folk music or style of musical performance? If change and identity are simply matters of choice, how far can one go toward choosing one's own folk music? Some means of moderating musical change might instead make the process of choice and musical acculturation more manageable, indeed possible at all. Much of that moderation takes place because of the presence of cultural boundaries.

The first type of folk music to lend itself readily to the study of cultural boundaries was that of immigrant groups. In recent decades theories of immigrant-group culture have proliferated, often ascribing considerable creativity to the group in its choice and maintenance of cultural boundaries. Previous studies, however, admitted relatively little creativity. The focus of many studies was actually on the core, with cultural boundaries admitted as defense mechanisms generally in retreat toward the core. Folk music of the immigrant group was a simple matter: it accompanied the group from the old country, and it remained as long as the boundaries were sufficient buttresses against the outside. The boundaries, however, had to be sure and steadfast over time.

As a corollary of *Kulturkreislehre*, a significant body of German folk music research turned to the study of *Sprachinseln* (speech islands). Folklore and folk music survived in these islands, isolated as they presumably were from the outside world. In most of these studies, survival bore primary witness to the strength of cultural boundaries. The Gottschee colony of Austrians in northern Yugoslavia, for example, maintained a tradition of folk music with relatively little change from the fourteenth century well into the nineteenth century (Brednich and Suppan 1969). When retention became so complete that it existed outside the boundaries of external society, "marginal survival" was said to have characterized the culture of the immigrant group. Thus the music of the Amish in North America has changed at an extremely slow pace because of the completeness with which the group is separated—musically as well as culturally—from mainstream society (Hostetler 1980:225–30 and Nettl 1957). Were survival to be the prevailing result of sustained division from the outside, cultural boundaries would have to obviate, rather than enable, change.

In most modern nations ethnic groups do not exist in isolation from each other. The conglomerate culture that results from a multiethnic society, pluralism, reflects the multitude of strategies for change and acculturation that its various groups undergo. Pluralism is only possible if the boundaries separating ethnic groups exhibit flexibility and permeability, if the exchange of members and culture across the boundaries does not tear them down (Barth 1969:14). Folk music, therefore, is not simply the practice and property of a single ethnic group, but it may have very different functions when the settings for its performance shift. The same musical ensemble may perform both inside and outside the ethnic group; it may perform in settings in which ethnicity is simply taken for granted and in those that demand a clear statement about ethnic values to those who are at best vaguely familiar with the ethnic group, as, for example, on the stage of a folk festival that promulgates a new "theme" each year.

The flexibility of boundaries makes possible the negotiation of different concepts of folk music style, repertory, and function. In many areas of pluralistic culture folk musicians encounter audiences that may differ considerably from performance to performance. The profile of one audience may be that of the ethnic community of the performer; another audience may contain a mixture from several of the ethnic groups in an area; still another might consist only of members from a community completely unlike that of the performer.

When performers who are specialists or professionals successfully meet the contrasting musical demands of these audiences, it is because of their ability to recognize the cultural boundaries, whether delimiting or expansive, and to locate each performance accordingly. In many areas of the Middle East, such specialists as the ᶜasheq (literally lover, but with many other meanings) expand their repertories not only to appeal to diverse ethnic groups but also to circumvent a wide range of other cultural and religious restraints (cf. Blum 1972 and Reinhard 1975). The result for such specialists is often a creative expansion of their own repertory, as well as that of the area or region in which they actively perform.

In extreme southwestern Wisconsin, one of the most creative folk music specialists is Charles Bannen, an octogenarian Irish-American farmer. Having lived his entire life in an area of ethnic pluralism, Bannen performs, alone or with other musicians, in virtually every performance context found in the area.

Two forms of creativity are evident in the tradition Bannen maintains as a specialist. First, from a core of Irish and Irish-American songs, Bannen has expanded his repertory to include a wealth of songs from other ethnic groups and American social institutions: churches, house parties, dances, and folk festivals. His repertory now ranges widely, from railroad songs to German dance tunes (which he occasionally performs in scatted versions) to nineteenth-century Protestant hymns (Bohlman 1980:171). Second, Bannen frequently creates new versions of the songs in his repertory by shifting musical aspects that serve as boundary markers. Thus Irish songs are rendered less Irish by removing certain types of embellishment (ibid.:176–78).

A somewhat more extreme result of Bannen's boundary awareness is the combination of two versions in a single perfomance, most often leaving the seam between the versions—the symbolic representation of the boundary—clearly intact. I recorded a version Bannen performed of "Streets of Laredo" (known also as "Cowboy's Lament" and "Tom Sherman's Barroom") in 1977 (example 4). Bannen's performance combines two versions, one more common in the eastern United States, the other more common west of the Mississippi (cf. Thorp 1966:180 and Abrahams 1970:76–78). The boundary falls between phrases three and four of the first verse. Comparing the versions on each side of the boundary, it is clear that Bannen knows the common western version better; in fact, he sometimes performs the song with the melody of that version intact. Still, there are occasions when audiences prefer the eastern version, especially younger audiences for whom that version was more common in school songbooks. By building on the foundations of versions he knows better, Bannen marks the boundary between the innovative and the traditional in his repertory (cf. Will 1909 and Barry 1987:72–73).

The boundaries animating the creativity in Bannen's repertory reflect very different processes of group identification in a pluralistic region of the Midwest; concomitantly, the social bases of folk music are very different. At one level, ethnicity predominates; at another level, religion determines cultural boundaries; at still other levels, generational cohesion and the availability of technology shape the formation of musical repertories and styles. But the flexibility with which Bannen treats the folk music of the region is a function of his own creativity. Conversely, there are repertories of folk music in other traditions that do not depend on the creativity of individuals but rather on the accumulation of multiple stylistic boundaries that can (and often must) respond to a variety of influences that shape and reshape the repertory itself. Flexibility and change, therefore, may have been prerequisites for survival.

Folk music in the pre-Holocaust Jewish communities of Europe exhibited many of the characteristics of this high degree of internal boundary flexibility. This flexibility notwithstanding, the separation of different traditions, especially

The Streets of Laredo

Singer: Charles Bannen
♩ = 144 mm

Mt. Zion, Wisconsin
8 October 1977
Collected and transcribed by P. V. Bohlman

EXAMPLE 4

Jewish and non-Jewish, was clear. Folk songs of a religious nature, for example, frequently absorbed influences from a variety of non-Jewish and secular sources. New songs often resulted when well-known tunes were used to set Hebrew texts; occasionally, vernacular texts also entered the tradition on the coattails of borrowed tunes.

In Eastern Europe folk songs in both Hebrew and the vernacular Yiddish were fairly common, often resulting from earlier didactic use. One of the best-known examples of bilingual folk song is "Yavo adir" (May the mighty one come), the text of which addresses the joy attending the eventual arrival of the Messiah (Idelsohn 1967:392–93 and 402). One version of "Yavo adir" (example 5) retains the religious and linguistic boundaries of the common Eastern European version but changes the Yiddish sections to German ("Wer wird das sein?") and the Ashkenazic Hebrew to Sephardic pronunciation. These changes are the result of a protracted musical journey from Eastern Europe to Germany and then to Israel, where the singer immigrated in the late 1930s. The performance of "Yavo adir" transcribed here bears influences from each stage of the journey. Eastern European versions often utilize the minor mode, with evidence of Phrygian suggested (e.g., ibid.). The German-Israeli version, however, was sung in the major mode, with implications for harmonization clear at several points. If the melody is most likely baggage from journeying through Germany, the Sephardic Hebrew is unquestionably an Israeli influence, acquired as the singer learned modern Israeli Hebrew after immigration.

The evidence of multiple cultural boundaries in folk music, whether the result of performers' choices or a part of the tradition, usually testifies to considerable creativity in folk music. Such creativity has no doubt always been a force for change in folk music, but it is even more widespread in the folk music of industrialized and multiethnic societies. Here the very presence of cultural boundaries is more extensive, as are the choices necessary to negotiate them. But as these choices multiply, so do the processes of change and the varieties of folk music itself.

The Social Basis of Dialectic between Cultural Core and Boundaries

When different ethnic communities and social groups come into contact, the interrelation of cultural core and boundaries becomes more dynamic. As one is forced to recognize other traditions, one is more sharply aware of the characteristics of one's own. In an immigrant community of Hungarians in the United States, for example, awareness of what is American defines by contrast what is Hungarian. Moreover, the coexistence of these two traditions may yield the dialectical interaction that we term Hungarian-American, with its juxta-

Yavo adir

Singer: Erika Reis

Jerusalem, Israel
14 July 1982
Collected and transcribed by P. V. Bohlman

Translation

May the might one come to redeem us,
May the holy one come to save us,
May Elijah come to unite us,
That will the Messiah bring about, our righteous one.

EXAMPLE 5

Who will that be?
The Son of David, our Savior!
When will that be?
Soon, in our own days!
What will that be?

A day of joy, of jubilation, of happiness, of pleasure,
Joy, jubilation, happiness, pleasure,
Hallelujah!

EXAMPLE 5 (Cont.)

position of internal and external. The "oppositional process" of identity not only produces new patterns of group-formation; it also strengthens the role of folklore as a shared and common set of traditions (Dundes 1984:149). The result of this contact with other groups and the attendant awareness of other boundaries was once thought to be the erosion of characteristics distinguishing one group from another. More extensive studies of group identity over time, however, reveal the capacity of social communities to absorb differences across cultural boundaries and to incorporate these differences into the dialectic between core and boundary. Interpretations of this dialectic have proved it to be a remarkably creative force in shaping the social basis of communities, especially those within a larger complex society (Kirshenblatt-Gimblett 1983:42–43).

The mediation of internal and external influences on folk music may take the form of several complex processes. Some of them are most evident in the emergence of new groups or subgroups in society. The impact of other influences is most readily measurable in changes at the core and the boundaries; new repertories exemplify the former, new modes and venues for performance the latter. In modern societies these complex processes are all of a whole. As new subgroups form, repertories are reshaped; as musicians diversify their performance settings, they effectively negotiate cultural boundaries. In this section I shall concentrate on several components of this complex dialectic mediating the cultural core and boundaries. I draw for illustration largely from the folk music of ethnic groups because of the contrast they provide: on one hand, the social basis of an ethnic group has long been assumed to be fixed; on the other, closer scrutiny of ethnic folk music reveals that it does not conform to a static, preservationist model but undergoes rapid change because of the creativity that a multiethnic environment inevitably engenders.

When particular needs arise that require specific responses of identity from a group, choices are made to channel these responses through institutions. These responses, the "folklore of ethnicity" (Danielson 1977 and Stern 1977), often result when an ethnic group chooses to express its self-perceived ethnicity for certain occasions but finds no reason to do so for other occasions. The process of making these choices is sometimes called cultural foregrounding (Kirshen-blatt-Gimblett 1983:43–44) or situational use of ethnicity (Royce 1982:18); the mechanism making this process possible is the social institution. For the most part, expressive behavior that is identified as appropriate for institutionalization normally receives a considerable investment of time and symbolic value from the group. German immigrant groups, for example, often use the singing society as the fundamental institution for the performance of folk music. In many areas of the American Midwest, this institutionalization of the singing society en-compassed other areas of musical activity. The singing society might, for ex-ample, supply many of the performers for local operetta; it might maintain an accompanying instrumental ensemble, which in turn performed elsewhere, not infrequently for non-German functions (Bohlman 1982:26–27). For subsequent generations of choristers the folk song traditions of the singing society provided a means of contact with symbols of German culture that may not have been readily available in the home or school. The institution of the singing society thus strengthened German ethnicity within the community and in groups out-side the community by intensifying awareness of German traditions and by providing a way for outsiders to participate in German musical life.

A primary vehicle for institutionalization is technology. Printing was one of the first technological media to influence folk music. Even from the earliest endeavors to print folk music in one form or another, two distinct directions characterized the institutionalizing impact of printing. The first produced what were essentially new songs by printing texts on broadsides and broadsheets and referring to tunes current in oral tradition. Consolidation most often re-sulted from the second use of printing. One form of the consolidating influence was the anthology, whereby a regional tradition was published in representative examples, that is to say, with boundaries clearly evident. For immigrant com-munities anthologies often served as the primary means of establishing a shared repertory and its related practices. This was the case among many Northern and Central European immigrant groups in the Midwest. Songbooks circulated within these groups, often published by a central ethnic publishing firm. Ac-cordingly, local differences in musical style, dialect, and musical repertory diminished as the songs in these books became representative of the second and third generations.

The institutionalization of ethnic folk music demonstrates considerable re-silience and the ability to change. Technological developments that influence other areas of musical activity may also alter the ways in which folk music is institutionalized. Recording technology, for example, was a primary—in some areas *the* primary—means of maintaining a vital tradition of ethnic folk music in North America throughout much of the twentieth century (Gronow 1982). More recently, the cassette recording has exerted a tremendous influence on musical traditions worldwide (Wallis and Malm 1984). Although some critics blame technology for transforming active folk music traditions into passive ones, within which most members of the ethnic group content themselves with a small, homogeneous sampling, a less pessimistic counterargument recognizes the potential for technology to expose larger audiences to a greater diversity of music. Moreover, recordings, as well as printed sources, play a vital role in the technologizing of oral tradition: musicians commonly learn new pieces directly from a record or tape cassette.

The institutions of ethnic culture do not simply reaffirm tradition from within; they may also strengthen ethnicity by allowing and then controlling the mixture of a group's traditions with those of other groups and external society in general. In studying "Ukrainian country music" Robert B. Klymasz observed a community of Canadian immigrants that freely utilized country-and-western music—a genre clearly representative of mainstream, English-speaking North American society—to revitalize Ukrainian music traditions. Although certain compromises in the active practice of the Ukrainian folk music tradition had to be made, these usually resulted in the emergence of new ways of keeping the tradition alive. The recording of Ukrainian country music, therefore, "exploits sound in order to process, codify, store and transmit the ethnic experience in a form that can be repeated over and over again as a sort of passive, psychic activity" (Klymasz 1972:373).

Folk festivals also serve as an institutional mechanism whereby ethnicity is made manageable. Many folk festivals reduce the active process of ethnic identification to several common denominators, most commonly food, dress, and folk music. The boundaries of these common denominators are carefully controlled, thereby ensuring a democratic pluralism while maintaining the necessary proviso of manageability. The size of food booths, for example, is often uniform. Musical performances may likewise be uniform, with each ethnic group performing a medley that lasts for a prescribed period and choosing from limited dance forms and musical genres—perhaps circle dances and harvest songs—that all groups presumably share. The differences between groups that could perform for hours and those that do well to prepare fifteen minutes are minimized by the festival. The history of many festivals starting after World War II shows steadily growing participation of new groups, with relatively little attrition by older groups. The folk festival has therefore succeeded in shoring up some preexistent boundaries, reinscribing others that had ceased to function as such, and ensuring permeability by sanctioning only those expressive genres that were easily visible and exchangeable across boundaries (cf. Dyen and Bohlman 1985, Haritan 1980, and Forry 1986).

Toward New Social Bases for Folk Music

Folklorists commonly assert that folklore is a function of shared identity. This assertion carries with it a further assumption, that the social basis of a group sharing folklore is flexible, subject to virtually any conditions that can produce a shared identity. One would more reluctantly accept parallel claims for folk music. Is folk music a function of shared identity? If "the first test a folklorist could make of membership in a folk group is the members' awareness of shared folklore" (Brunvand 1986:41), could the folk music scholar extend the same test to shared music? One could argue that the subculture of British punkers shares a folklore; but would one designate their shared music folk music? Symphony orchestra musicians share many common factors specifically related to music, but they are not infrequently oblivious to genres others call folk music. In these cases we would not question the existence of an adequate social basis for folklore, but we are harder pressed to proclaim this social basis adequate for folk music.

Throughout this chapter, nevertheless, I have not questioned what I consider an appropriate association of folk music with social basis, either that pertaining to a sense of place or that pertaining to a sense of community. And I have admitted to this social basis considerable flexibility, especially the ability to change in response to external influences and internal specialist-performers. Taken together, the changes that I have admitted can yield a social basis very different from that yielded by earlier theories about communal participation and dispassionate reproducibility of shared behavior. This call for a new conceptualization of folk music's relation to different social bases is therefore consistent with the broader understanding of folk music posited throughout this book.

The social basis of folk music is constantly in flux. That flux, however, is not freely determined by any choices made by any group perceiving self-identity. It is, instead, a flux that results from the dynamic interrelation of core and boundaries. This dialectic couples persistent change with conservative tendencies that stem change. Necessitating the dialectic is folk music's essentially performative nature. As a genre of expressive behavior, folk music must be learned, and some form of repetition is requisite. Folk music cannot be acquired at will; it restricts, to some extent, the openness to choose and share identity.

If the social basis of folk music changes according to certain constraints, it changes nonetheless. In this chapter I have examined some of the processes that make change possible but channel it in certain directions. The geographic basis of folk music has not disappeared, but it has effectively migrated from rural to urban models, from simple to complex settings. Here, new boundaries arise; the influences on musical genres are greater, but no urban musical grayout is in sight (see Reyes Schramm 1982 and Nettl 1985:76–78). Modernized social institutions, ranging from singing societies to recordings, reformulate the core traditions but rarely, if ever, eradicate them. These social institutions and the folk traditions they shape are determined by processes of group identity that mediate the choices of identity necessary for maintaining a specialized genre of folklore such as folk music. Such processes, furthermore, enable a community to choose whether the social basis of its folk music will reflect the ascribed pluralism of the folk festival or the embellishment of mainstream popular culture. In the modern world the folk music of every social community confronts a tremendous quantity and diversity of influences. Yet because of its complex relation to the patterns of identity forming the infrastructure of the community, folk music continues to undergird a social basis that animates change and directs tradition.

FIVE

The Folk Musician

The creative process is not one begun and
finished by a single individual; it is spread
over many individuals and generations, and it
never comes to an end as long as the tradition is alive.

George Herzog (1949–50:1034)

Let it be literally cried from the house tops
that the folk singer is a personality, an individual, and most of all a creative artist.

Phillips Barry (1961:76)

Until recently, many scholars believed that folk music was voiceless. It was to
be devoid of individual personality. It should lack the marks of distinction that
revealed the shaping influences of creative talent. If *das Volk dichtet,* specific
folk musicians did not. Were folk music a force of cultural and national unity,
it could not also change at the behest of a few unusual individuals or those
recognized as musical specialists. The timeless quality of folk music, too, ob-
viated any possibility of outstanding individuals. After all, folk music was a
measure of generations, not the estimation of one person's lifetime.

The long-standing failure of folk music scholarship to take account of individual creativity is perhaps the most visible testimony to the undercurrent of
conservatism that has saturated many of our most entrenched concepts of folk
music. Considerations of cultural and musical change, for example, muddy this
undercurrent and thus are too often channeled into the nondescript pools of
popular music. Even the themes organizing the opening chapters of this book
admit to the lingering traces of this conservative strain in my own thinking,
whether through searching for the logic and order attending the origins and
transmission of folk music or in seeking the patterns of cohesion that bind human
and musical aggregates together. The folk musician, at least in many societies
and genres, challenges the implicit order that motivates many theories of folk

music by composing new songs that enter oral tradition, serving as a conduit to traditions outside the community, making choices about a repertory to be performed in specific settings, and specializing in certain genres or as an instrumentalist. Change is inevitable.

But if change is inevitable, it also may fall into patterns or yield social norms. And these patterns and norms may conform to the constraints of community and tradition. They prevent the folk musician's individuality from being random, just as they provide criteria for community response to creativity. Concepts of community and musician, therefore, need not be mutually exclusive. Indeed, considered together, they focus other contrasting concepts, such as stability and change or cultural core and boundaries. Investigation of the characteristics that determine the individual's role in folk music also recasts the concept of the social basis of folk music; the group is not disregarded but seen instead in relation to the ways particularity and individuality function to shape the whole. Similarly, the folk musician's creativity is not anathema to tradition but rather a process animating tradition.

The Folk Musician as Tradition-Bearer

The folk musician described by much earlier scholarship played a paradoxical role. "The folk" comprised all individuals in a society, and folk song issued from the mouths and souls of all. This egalitarian distribution of folk music ipso facto made it impossible to single out specific individuals as exceptional performers. Folk music was defined by ubiquitous musicality, never by the creative impetus of individual personalities. George Herzog merely echoed the assumption of most scholars when he portrayed folk music through the prerequisite of widespread participation.

> Folk song is an art in which the average member of the group participates more generally than is the case with the cultivated music or literature of the city. Nearly everyone in a folk group knows songs and sings them, or at least listens to them and knows a good deal about them. On the many occasions at which singing is by a group, the less outstanding singers have ample opportunities for participating (Herzog 1949–50:1034).

Folk music was to be the art of everyman.

When concepts of folk music became more complex, accumulating qualities of place, transmission, or social structure, these qualities perpetuated the voicelessness of folk music and the paradox of individual participation. With the sharpening of the urban-rural dichotomy, it became necessary to perceive rural society as a setting in which all people could and did participate in folk music. Rural society thus became even more idealized, urban society more resistant to true folk music. Accordingly, musical specialists were absent in the rural setting but proliferated as the result of urban influences (ibid.).

From this perspective the origins of folk music should also lie in a nonspecialized society. A number of theoretical variants arose from the assumption of universal participation in the origin of folk music. These variants ranged from the association of folk music with play to the claim that people working together spontaneously generated song as a means of easing their labors (Barry 1961:59–61). The ballad theories of Francis Gummere argued polemically for the origins of ballad in the communality of "dancing throngs," with their natural transformation of movement into dramatic situations and rhythmic patterns (Gummere 1907:71–85 and 1961:20–29). It is hardly surprising that theories of group origin should produce a fair amount of literature steeped in ideology and bias. Most often, this literature, like its precursors, remains at the level of the abstract, obtaining largely in idealized "preindustrial" societies (e.g., Lomax 1968:170). Occasionally, it promulgates misconceptions that blind researchers to the complexity of certain musical cultures, causing them to argue for the special value of musical communality. The impulse to idealize has been especially persistent in studies of African music, and only very recently has more localized ethnography revealed considerable musical specialization in many, if not most, African societies (e.g., Merriam 1982:321–56).

The tendency of folk music research devoid of individual musicians is to homogenize time and tradition, to reduce them along with the role of folk musicians to an innocuous sameness. The older a tradition, the fewer the individual influences. Should a tradition have primordial wellsprings, the absence of composition at the point of inception would further justify the absence of recognizable musicians over time. And so transmission exists sui generis. It does not require individual efforts to provide it with energy. Transmission, then, acquires a preeminent position. The human role in the maintenance of this position is one of passing music on to subsequent generations, ideally without introducing any change, even if it means suppressing individuality. The folk musician should be merely a tradition-bearer. The tradition-bearer generally has specific attributes that define his or her nonrole. First, the folk musician exhibits unflagging respect for tradition, which is by its nature inviolable. What the folk musician receives, the folk musician transmits. Second, the folk musician is dispassionate, maintaining a certain emotional distance from the text of a song or the performance style of instrumental music. This might even result in flexibilty of intonation or rhythm (Herzog 1949–50:1041). Finally, the folk musician keeps tradition alive by performing, not by an objective knowledge of its bounds or the function it fulfills throughout a given society.

This lack of objective knowledge serves also to purify tradition, for it implies that the folk musician does not have an active awareness of external traditions or the possibilities for change.

Ironically, albeit appropriately, the concept of folk musician as tradition-bearer appears first in studies that take special note of musicians who are not simply indistinguishable threads in the fabric of folk music. These musicians, instead, stand out because they are unusual. They catch the eye of the fieldworker and attract subsequent visits by other scholars. They make the job of collecting easier because they know more songs and more variants than others in a community. They are the individuals to whose door one is first directed when entering a community. They are the key informants around whom regional anthologies are built, the Emma Dusenburys and Almeda Riddles (cf. Belden 1973, Randolph 1980, and Abrahams 1970). A background of voiceless tradition-bearers may still exist, but there emerges from this background a particular type of folk musician whose activities illumine the rest of the community in new ways, casting up new details and putting other exceptional individuals in a more distinct chiaroscuro. If dispassionate, voiceless tradition-bearing does not disappear, another form of tradition joins it, this one accompanied by folk musicians conscious of the unique contributions they stand to make.

The Folk Musician and Performance

Several related reasons account for the greater attention individual folk musicians have received in recent years. As fieldwork becomes more intensive, the variation within culture becomes more striking, appearing normative in its distribution. In general, recent folk music research has concentrated on smaller groups and communities and concerned itself less with fleshing out preconceived notions of national repertoires or monolithic corpora. The focus of much research has shifted from the general to the specific, from predetermined pattern to thick description in which pattern results from a multiplicity of diverse details (Geertz 1973:3–30). For an expressive behavior that, like music, is temporal in nature, detail is inevitably a function of performance. Recognizing this function produces a fundamentally different view of folk music. It forces a reformulation of concern for prototypes, taking instead the plethora of variants as commonplace. The tradition of folk music is therefore not simply a question of whether a song exists in a particular region, or how close the versions of that song are to the song's appearance in a given anthology. Instead, tradition embraces all versions of a song, which in turn becomes the sum of all its performances.

To concentrate on performance it is necessary to recognize fully the role of the folk musician. Each performance is the expressive act of an individual or a group of individuals, and that expressive act reflects the interrelation of the performer and the tradition. The performance poses many questions about that interrelation, questions that only the musician is fully capable of answering. How does the folk musician learn a particular song? From whom? What personal stories relate to the musician's concept of the song? Was this performance an appropriate context for the song? What is the range of appropriate contexts? Does this version replicate others, or are there innovative elements? Would it be appropriate to add to or alter the piece? To compose a new song in its stead? The answers to such questions contribute to a more complete understanding of tradition, not simply a justification of tradition. They place the folk musician at the center of tradition and insist that only through the analysis of performance can a broad understanding of tradition be reached.

The performative aspects of tradition, while drawing attention to the folk musician, reveal ways whereby expressive behavior that previously seemed exceptional may have normative forces tempering it. By studying many performances of upstate New York singer Dorrance Weir, Henry Glassie observed that the composition of new verses for "Take That Night Train to Selma" was guided by audience response. If a verse met with audience approval, always signified by laughter, it stayed in the song; if approval was not forthcoming during performance, verses quickly exited (Glassie 1970:29–30). Performance was also essential to the satiric song tradition in the Canadian Maritimes and the American Northeast (Ives 1964). The use of folk song to exert power or mark interaction with neighbors might at first glance appear to require more invention and particularity than any tradition could tolerate. Instead, it was a tradition that many song-makers practiced, some more effectively than others. Those who excelled in the tradition, such as Larry Gorman, did so because they were masters of ad hoc creativity and could adapt the tradition through performance to the need for satire (ibid.:180–81). The key to understanding the tradition, therefore, was seeing what sort of pastiche individual performances yielded.

The folk musician uses performance to express an understanding of the relation between stability and change. Some performances may incorporate more techniques that bring about change; others ensure stability. The musician's role, therefore, is not one of simply bearing tradition via repetition or, in contrast, willfully innovating. It can, and usually does, combine both, the ultimate balance depending on the audience, which is also an indispensable component of performance. Like individual folk musicians, audiences manipulate the balance of stability and change. During the performance, the audience's response may draw attention to the violation of traditional expectations or it may encourage creativity. The skillful performer, too, knows from the composition of his audience what stylistic and social boundaries can or cannot be crossed. Each performance, therefore, becomes a metaphor for the folk musician's relation to tradition and its social and musical bases.

Creativity vs. Representation: The Individual's Role in Traditional Change

Many discussions of folk music assume that tradition eschews creativity. Correlatively, many histories of Western art music depart not at all from the nineteenth-century notion that change is essential if music is to develop with vigor and to respond to the social conditions of its day. Such contrasting assumptions about music would have the reader believe that creativity and tradition are mutually exclusive. These assumptions define music so narrowly as to reinforce the contrasting levels prescribing folk and art music in highly stratified societies. But assumptions they are. And as assumptions they require rather restricted views of how change occurs and who stimulates the processes of creativity. They rest on idealized models of tradition that belie the reality of the present and insist on relegating folk music to the past.

In their most basic form these assumptions place creativity at odds with representation—which I use here to mean a performance in which the musician intends to adhere to the piece as it was learned. In this polemical position, creativity and representation appear in a number of other conflicts, including the conflict between individualist and communalist views of society. The rudimentary argument posed by this conflict is that individual acts introduce change, whereas communal society stems change. A wide range of evidence, nevertheless, refutes this argument. Communal settings may, in fact, be quite tolerant of individual expression, and individuals may, in contrast, take great pains to conform. Genres that depend on individuality are sometimes bound to those that require concerted effort. Research by John Spitzer and Neal Zaslaw (1986) suggests that improvisation by individual musicians was an institutionalized practice of eighteenth-century orchestral performance. In other words, it was expected that ensemble players would use a communal setting to demonstrate individuality. This widespread practice, moreover, provides a radical contrast to the model of orderliness and decorum that cultural historians have preferred to see in the eighteenth-century Age of Enlightenment or the Classic Era in music history. Observing such different cultural phenomena as African society and jazz in the United States, Alan P. Merriam consistently argued that the "deviance" of certain musicians was normative in society (1982:330). Extreme individuality was thus the essential link to functional community social and aesthetic systems (Merriam 1979:19).

Creativity assumes many forms in folk music. Some musicians may exercise creative options in an intentional way, consciously attempting to introduce change, or at least variation, into traditional styles. For other folk musicians, creativity may be largely unintentional, even though the eventual result is widespread innovation and change. The reasons for unintentional creativity vary. Knowledge of the tradition may be incomplete, forcing the musician to draw from another stock of convenient techniques during performance. The musician may play in contrasting performance settings, some of which require relatively unfamiliar repertory; folk musicians performing widely in pluralistic regions may face such situations frequently. In these cases, the impulse toward change may not originate in the musician, but the attitudes of both musician and audience may demonstrate considerable tolerance for certain types of change that occur unintentionally. During the past century many areas of the Midwest have witnessed the growing use of instruments to accompany previously soloistic ethnic vocal repertories. Inevitably tied to this transformation has been the use of harmonization, usually the basic patterns found in much European art music of the eighteenth and nineteenth centuries. Harmonization not only imposes a new vocabulary on a traditional folk melody; it also forces a restructuring of the melody's syntax. In certain non-Western repertories, the encroachment of harmony has produced a preference for modal structures that lend themselves more easily to the vertical structures of harmonization. Often, these non-Western modes are those that resemble the Western major and minor modes most closely (Nettl 1985:37–40).

For many musicians, adherence to this new syntax is of considerably less importance than using chords in repetitive, standardized patterns regardless of form or harmonic implications in the melody. The performance of "Barbara Allen" (example 6) illustrates one possible manifestation of the unintentional creativity resulting from juxtaposing harmonization—in this case the chordal accompaniment at a reed organ—on a traditional melody. This common version of Child 84 uses a pentatonic scale, lacking fourth and seventh degrees that would make it modally major (cf. Seeger 1966:120–67). In this performance Charles Bannen expands the possible harmonization of one verse to encompass two verses. Accordingly, two types of change result. First, the melody acquires the leading tone (F sharp) of a G-Major scale, thereby directing the harmonic drive toward the tonic and replicating the third degree of the dominant triad in Bannen's harmonic pattern. Second, those places where melodic and harmonic syntax conflict result in the singing of certain pitches out of tune (marked here with arrows). At the beginning of the second verse, when Bannen sings B while playing a subdominant chord with its root on C—lacking in the pentatonic scale, but only a half step from B—he sings it sharp, in effect introducing a type of "blues note," which occurs at other similar points of syntactic juxtaposition (e.g., "against" in the second verse).

In the ethnically diverse areas of Wisconsin and northern Michigan that border Lake Superior, instrumental performance of many previously vocal repertories may well have become normative during the twentieth century (Leary 1984). Instrumental arrangements are common in such institutionalized genres as ethnic recordings and public dances, and the use of instruments with the concomitant introduction of harmonization is frequent in the home music-making of all ethnic groups in the area. Contemporary folk music tradition, thus, virtually demands that musical instruments serve as a conduit for unintentional creativity, that is, change. By examining a broad cross-section of the region's ethnic repertory, it is possible to identify various stages of unintentional creativity.

In an incipient stage (example 7), the Finnish-American accordion player applies harmonic patterns in a purely tactile manner. The syntax of the harmonization would work fairly well, were it not in the wrong mode, B-flat Major (the relative major, also using two flats) rather than g minor. Although the resulting harmonies may not sound "correct" to the outsider, they conform to the kinesthetic criterion that has made widespread introduction of harmony through instrumental music possible (for the significance of kinesthetic patterns in a Chinese instrumental tradition, see Yung 1984).

Barbara Allen

Singer: Charles Bannen   Mt. Zion, Wisconsin
$\quad$ ♩ = 76 mm   8 October 1977
Child Ballad 84   Collected by P.V. Bohlman

EXAMPLE 6 (cf. Bohlman 1980:178–80)

Such elements of unintentional creativity are again evident in extracts from the Finnish-American dance "Iitin Tiltu" (example 8). The modal conflict posed by juxtaposed harmonic patterns has now evolved into the presence of mixed modes, including the combination of major and minor chords on the tonic (I and i) and subdominant (IV and iv). More complex use of harmonic structures—for example, the frequent occurrence of chords in first inversion (e.g., I^6)—reflects the expansion of the innovative component of the Finnish-American musical vocabulary. Finally, the quantity and degree of melodic variation has increased in pace with harmonic complexity, thus signaling a complete transition to a stage in which creativity has become requisite and representation of prototypical versions extremely rare.

The inherent creativity of many folk music traditions represents a vast array of individual attitudes toward the balance of innovation and representation. Some musicians may use the possibilities of creativity as a means of expanding individual poetic license. In contrast, others may take a reactionary stance, recognizing in the processes of creativity a musical territory that violates tradition. Some may use creativity to concentrate audience response on the folk musician, while others successfully diffuse the importance of the individual by consciously sidestepping creativity. At the very least, creativity clearly delineates the various limits a tradition may have, and it does so by drawing attention to the folk musician's position vis-à-vis those limits.

The different types of creativity and the individual attitudes they represent

Muurarin Valssi (Mason's Waltz)

Accordionist: Reino Maki
♩ = 138 mm

Washburn, Wisconsin
1980–81
Collected by J.P. Leary
Transcribed by P.V. Bohlman

EXAMPLE 7 (cf. Leary 1986a:side 4, cut 1, and Leary 1986b:27)

Iitin Tiltu

Accordionist: Hugo Maki
♩ = 144 mm

Washburn, Wisconsin
1980–81
Collected by J.P. Leary
Transcribed by P.V. Bohlman

EXAMPLE 8 (cf. Leary 1986a:side 4, cut 3, and Leary 1986b:29)

form a continuum, with one end demanding faithful representation of the repertory and the other end permitting conscious innovation. Eleanor Long (1973) has proposed four typical responses of ballad singers to musical creativity that are suggestive of my somewhat expanded pattern for this continuum. At one extreme is *regulated creativity*, a process Long calls "perseverating," which characterizes a "ballad singer who insists upon faithful reproduction of his text" (ibid.:232). Even though accurate representation is the primary motivation for perseverating, it is nevertheless an active process, one that presumes that knowing how to effect faithful reproduction predicates conscious awareness of how and where departure from tradition takes place. At the other pole of the continuum is *ubiquitous creativity*, a process whereby willful departure from traditional constraints is the rule rather than the exception. Long sees this process, which she labels "confabulating," as a sort of loss of faithfulness, both to the tradition and to any version of it that the individual folk musician produces in a given performance (ibid.:232–33). I am less willing than Long to see wanton abandon as motivation for this extreme, for that would entail a failure to consider audience and cultural expectations, in other words, a complete departure from tradition itself. Even the most extreme creativity, I would suggest, is possible only with some tempering influences from tradition, some foundation that can serve as a reference for variation and change.

Individual choices play a greater or lesser role on the continuum, depending on to which extreme the folk musician is closer. Not far from the more conservative extreme is a process that might be labeled *discriminatory creativity*. In this process the musician may perform in a faithful manner but make certain choices that limit repertory or aspects of performance. Ozark singer Almeda

Riddle, for example, exhibited discriminatory creativity by choosing to sing only folk songs that were complete and those with "classic" value. This process of discrimination resulted from personal decisions and the incorporation of external values: complete songs usually were songs with a narrative that made sense, and classic songs usually included corpora that collectors and scholars had canonized, such as the Child ballads (Abrahams 1970:156–57).

Awareness of external influences and values plays a somewhat greater role in the category that I call, drawing on Long, *rationalized creativity* (1973:233). This process relates to the folk musician's ability to adapt traditional material to external values and contexts. The musician functions as a mediator, using a supposedly neutral store of texts and musical materials under new circumstances. Rationalized creativity is similar to what James Porter calls "a feature of style that transcends the harder sanctions on meaning and relevance when the local context is exchanged for the exoteric" (1985:327). Musicians exhibiting this quality, like Scottish ballad singers Jeannie Robertson and Belle Stewart, whose creative prowess Porter has studied with singular thoroughness, possess a "knowledge and power . . . to move all who listen, whether native to the tradition or not" (ibid.; see also Porter 1976 and 1986).

Extensive contact outside the folk musician's own community may engender a still more creative process, one in which new material is adapted to traditional formulae. *Integrative creativity*, then, combines old and new materials in specific ways, so that repertories and styles are in effect altered, but in ways consistent with the expectations of diverse audiences (Long 1973:233–34). Integrative creativity lies relatively close to the extreme of ubiquitous creativity, but differs because the integrative musician is clearly a specialist: he stands out against the traditional background because of a special willingness to identify and tap appropriate new material. It is this process that distinguished Maine songmaker Joe Scott, whose role as a folk musician has been chronicled by Edward D. Ives (1978). Scott actually combined two traditions—the Anglo-American ballad and the nineteenth-century popular sentimental song—as a technique of composing new songs that appealed to broad audiences on several levels. Ives summarizes Scott's integrative creativity:

> Given his chosen field of expression, he was a master not only in the sense that he could work extremely well *within* the tradition, but also in the sense that he went beyond it, showing considerable originality in his inventive use of models, his combining of popular and folk traditions (especially in his use of the language of sentimental song in balladry), and his leisurely and elaborate style of development. Had the tradition continued in "expected" fashion, we might well have been able to show how Joe altered its direction by virtue of his work becoming part of it and furnishing new models (Ives 1978:412; the parentheses are Ives's).

This continuum is meant to suggest the tremendous range of relationships between individual creativity and a society's expectation of adherence to tradition. Rather than being mutually exclusive, creativity and representation of tradition are mutually dependent; they define each other by their balance and interaction. Creativity depends on tradition to give it direction; tradition becomes flaccid and moribund without creativity to animate it. Maintaining this balance is the folk musician. Indeed, the ability and care with which the musician sustains the balance becomes also the measure of the musician's skill and specialized role in society.

Specialization and the Folk Musician

Folk music is totally without vitality unless performed. It cannot survive only as an artifact. The folk musician must be more than a curator. Nor can passive audiences make a tradition. The folk musician invests time in the maintenance of the tradition—to learn, to practice, to perform. Folk music may be inseparable from daily labors, but it more frequently accents or punctuates those labors. And so too in the life of a community, folk music signals a departure from the usual, a moment that articulates the aesthetic and social values undergirding community. Performance of folk music is therefore a specialized practice. As such, it takes place in the hands of specialists, whom the community has designated not because of a passive willingness to bear the tradition forth but because of a particular skill or designated social role that provides the creative energy required to keep the tradition vital.

The determinants of specialization in folk music differ greatly from society to society. In some cultures the musician gains prestige; in others he may lose prestige. Some communities reward folk musicians with a small payment in recompense for the rendering of specific services; others designate professionals and provide them with full-time support. In those societies where many members participate, there may be only a few roles—for example, playing the largest instrument—that distinguish the specialists; when participation is relatively sparse, it may be a specialty simply to perform publicly at all. Value and aesthetic judgments, too, appear universally as markers of specialization (cf. Seeger 1977:324–25). Insisting that a musician is, by definition, a specialist, Merriam observed "that in all societies individuals exist whose skill at making music is recognized in some way as being superior to that of other individuals so that they are called upon, or simply take their 'rightful' place, in musical situations" (1964:124).

To understand how a folk musician becomes a specialist or exercises a differentiated musical role, it behooves us to observe different types of musical specialization. In this section I sketch several of the ways in which specialist status obtains in the folk music of different cultures. These categories are not meant as discrete or exclusive, and in practice musicians may draw upon several categories to achieve specialist status; a musician recognized as a social deviant, for example, may also perform on a musical instrument and receive regular payment for doing so. The categories therefore suggest the complex processes determining the specialization of a folk musician. These processes result from a society's conceptualization of the folk musician's role and the individual's achievement of that role. Even in the most extreme forms of that role, society and individual reach a consensus with regard to the acceptable limits of musical behavior. Thus, the role of the folk musician may in some cases be conspicuous, while in others barely evident. In all cases, however, some form of specialization marks that role.

Wide distribution of specialization. Earlier models of folk music in isolated rural areas often implied an ideal of all people participating in all music. Such folk music would therefore lack specialization. Models of this sort were further predicated on such notions as "primitive society" in which lack of artistic differentiation presumably resulted from an essentially human egalitarianism. Closer ethnographic observation, however, uncovered some basic conflicts, even in the most idealized renderings of these models. Not everyone sang the same music; not all music was known to everyone. Musical life was specialized in some ways. Repertories paralleled the differentiation of culture according to sex or age. Women more commonly sang lullabies; specific musical roles accompanied rites of passage. Just as division of labor existed on some scale, so too were musical roles distributed according to certain patterns. One can speak of musical specialization in such societies as widely distributed. Specialization exists, but for the most part it characterizes subgroups rather than individuals. These subgroups may originate from other social activities, but their organization may also be musical, as in the case of drumming ensembles in West Africa. This category covers a broad range of possibilities, many of which are distinguished by fairly widespread participation in musical activities. Participation, in this sense, extends to the processes that bring about musical specialization, enhancing its relation to other social activities.

The specialization of skills. Various factors, most of them embedded in a society's conceptualization of music, identify certain skills as specialties. Some specialties are relatively abstract, labeled, perhaps, as talents, whereas others may take the form of material phenomena. A folk musician may be born with a skill or may acquire it after years of directed effort. It is this difference that Merriam describes with the terms *ascribed* and *acquired* musical roles

(1964:130–33). Ascribed skills may predominate in some cultures, acquired in others; but both draw attention to individual musicians and ensure the perpetuation of specialization.

One skill basic to oral transmission is memory. The genres of folk music differ considerably with regard to the demands placed on sheer memory. Many genres are largely repetitive, whereas others require a seemingly vast store of memorized details and techniques. Genres requiring skill in memorization tend not to be as widely distributed as those that are highly repetitive. Accordingly, epic singers in the Balkans command remarkable memories and are recognized by society for this skill, both by means of attaching some reputation to the singers and by making it possible for the most skillful to make epic-singing a profession. The performance of musical instruments also requires measurable skills that frequently receive some reward from society. Instrumental skill is apparently one of the most basic denominators of musical specialization in some societies. Among the Basongye of Zaire the five major classifications of musician relate directly to instrumental skills or lack thereof (Merriam 1982:329). In contemporary Anglo-American folk music, fiddling contests have increasingly come to rank musicians according to their instrumental skills, bringing, of course, commensurate rewards as further designation of this form of specialization.

Skills may be relatively normative or highly exceptional; in most folk music, skill has both normative and exceptional qualities. Memory may generally be a skill in oral transmission, although certain types of memory may be more highly valued. Among the Venda in southern Africa, participation in music requiring quite diverse skills is normative (Blacking 1957:45–46). Acquisition of at least rudimentary instrumental skills is desirable in many parts of the United States. Skill, like other aspects of folk music specialization, requires recognition from both society and the musician. Each makes diverse choices about those skills that have special meaning, but such choices are inevitably a part of identifying the panoply of musical roles in culture.

The specialization of elevated or important social functions. Few societies lack ways of quickly identifying those musicians who perform important social functions. The folklorist frequently witnesses this process of social identification when engaging in fieldwork. Upon asking in a community about musicians, it becomes quickly evident whom the community regards as "good," and not infrequently informants identify specifically the social function that qualifies these musicians as "good." One may play well at dances; another may sing all the "old" songs; still another may perform "new" songs at a nearby radio station. These musicians are a community's designated specialists. Their specialty is not necessarily an aesthetic or technical quality, but a recognition of those social functions that a community wishes to maintain; their performances thus symbolize and reinforce the patterns of social organization that the community values the most (Szwed 1970:150–51).

It is not uncommon for communities to institutionalize musical specialists according to social function. Religious institutions, for example, delegate specialists to organize a wide range of musical activities that often spill over into secular life. In some cases, musicians actually function as a priesthood, binding religious activity to musical expression. There are other cases in which musicians are identified by extramusical traits, which then assume the characteristic of a specialty vis-à-vis musical institutions. Some observers believe that the blind are often channeled toward musical specialization, citing such cases as the *goze* of Japan who may actually have been recruited on the basis of blindness (Harich-Schneider 1959:56 and Merriam 1964:132). The Bauls, a Bengali religious sect with distinctive musical practices, fulfill different social functions, depending on whether their audiences are Bauls or other Bengalis, for whom the Bauls and their music represent the leveling of religious and caste restrictions (Capwell 1986:10). The Bauls themselves absorb this social stance into their own culture, while outsiders, through the influence of Rabindranath Tagore and others, have transmuted specifically Baul themes into Bengali art and culture (ibid.:20-32). In Bengali society, then, the music of the Bauls, though no longer just Bengali per se, becomes the explicit symbol of an abstract social context that is both idealized and disdained.

Deviance. When individual musicians function in ways that the bulk of a society would never sanction for itself, the specialization of these musicians manifests deviance. Deviance, in this usage, does not imply extrasocietal behavior. Deviants are, instead, necessary to society, for they specialize in forms of cultural expression that could become dysfunctional were they to become commonplace. Merriam found that Basongye society was unanimous in its condemnation of the behavior of deviant musical specialists, who engaged in many, if not most, of those activities the Basongye deemed unacceptable. Just as unanimous was the assertion that the social order would disintegrate without these musical specialists.

> Non-musicians react with genuine seriousness to the possible loss of musicians, saying that "life in a village without musicians is not to be considered." Non-musicians and musicians alike speak of leaving Lupupa Ngye were no musicians present, and such a reaction is extremely strong, for the people are closely tied to the village by powerful and multifaceted bonds of kinship, economics, and emotion. The importance of the musician to the other members of society, then, is extremely high (Merriam 1979:3).

The extent of deviance depends on both social and individual attitudes toward musical behavior. Thus, if specialized deviance is widespread in a culture, it may mean that music has a low status but that social norms still accord great importance to music by delegating specialists as musicians. In many Islamic societies, disfavor and proscription greet music-making. Music does not, however, disappear from these societies, which continue to demonstrate their need for music by tolerating various forms of specialized deviance. Outsiders, especially minorities, have often assumed a disproportionately high percentage of musical activities. Certain types of musician have deflected criticism by diversifying within the bounds of their specialty, thus making it difficult to identify them as "just a musician" in any single genre of performance (Shiloah 1974:52). The performance of certain genres traditionally took place in settings that bore a deviant stigma—for example, coffeehouses—thus separating music from the disapproval of more orthodox Islamic society.

It is important to remember that deviance is a cultural category. The successful deviant musician carefully observes the limits placed on his specialty by society; to step beyond these limits would, in effect, terminate his livelihood. Existence of deviance also allows society to maintain musical activities that it cannot condone but that are nevertheless indispensable. The interaction between society and specialized musical deviance therefore forms a complementary relationship. One depends on the other, with the end result that musicians function in an intricate web of specialization.

Communication. The specialization of the folk musician usually proffers mobility, both literal and figurative. This mobility brings the musician into contact with new forms of aesthetic expression, a wide range of social settings, and, rather often, groups other than the immediate one of which the musician is a member. The development of instrumental specialists in European secular music, with its roots first apparent in the Middle Ages, was paralleled by many different communicative roles, ranging from the wandering minstrel to the civic musician representing his city at festivals and public events in other cities (Schwab 1982:15). This broadening of contacts and influences affects the musician's attitudes, activities, and repertories, all of which gain a necessary flexibility augmenting other aspects of specialization. That change results is inevitable, for the folk musician in different situations is confronted with choices. That the musician communicates these choices and the concomitant change to audiences is also inevitable.

In some societies special recognition accrues to certain folk music specialists because of the communicative function. The narrative technique favored by many broadside composers is that of recounting and elaborating a type of news. It is not just the manner of producing songs that distinguishes many broadside composers and performers; so also do dress, instrument, and position in the urban marketplace for professionals like the German *Bänkelsänger* or Bulgarian *panairdžijski pevec* (Roth and Roth 1985:343–44). The more expansive world-view of many broadside composers becomes the explicit motivation for musical specialization.

The modes of expression in which this communicative function is evident may be aesthetic or social in nature. Extreme forms of social creativity can accord the musician outsider status, which both signals the fact that the musician is not a member of the community and enhances the ability with which the musician responds to change because of the license outsider status affords. In various Middle Eastern contexts outsider status is cultivated by community and musician alike to circumvent the possibility of negative responses to music-making (cf. Lortat-Jacob 1984 and Schuyler 1984). Claiming that the music one experiences is not really the community's in effect disavows local responsibility.

Musicians whose communicative function centers on aesthetic aspects often narrow, rather than expand, cultural distance. Dan Gruetzmacher, a German-American concertina player from rural northern Wisconsin, exemplifies the folk musician who has specialized in mastering the musical dialects of ethnic old-time genres. This specialty allows Gruetzmacher and his orchestra to perform for most of the large ethnic groups represented in the Upper Midwest, even though he claims as his preferred style the "Dutchman" music associated with German-American communities. If his audience is Slovenian-American, he communicates a Slovenian style; if it is Polish-American, he slips easily into a Polish melos. This communicative flexibility means that Gruetzmacher can play in many more ethnic settings than he could if he were content only with "Dutchman" style. In turn, his musical specialization has gained him considerable fame, with the result that his economic base too has broadened (Bohlman 1985 and Martin et al.:1986).

Professionalism. Professionalism results when music becomes virtually a full-time activity for the folk musician. Music provides a way of making a living. Although various degrees and forms of specialization bring about an exchange of goods and services to reward music-making, there are still specialists in many societies who use music as the primary means of livelihood. Until recently, many folk music scholars regarded professionalism with reprobation: folk music was, by definition, nonprofessional. Professionalism was seen as an urban phenomenon, and it produced a distinction between concert-giver and concertgoer that was not possible among rural groups, whose performers and audiences usually melded into one (Herzog 1949–50:1034). But rural cultures, too, had professional folk musicians, and in many cases they performed within traditions of great age (Roth and Roth 1985:343 and Lord 1960). Moreover, different types of professionalism might well coexist in rural and urban areas of the same culture (Roth and Roth 1985:344).

Professionalism is not only a phenomenon of folk music in urbanized or modernized contexts. Merriam has proposed that professionalism, rather than measuring financial recompense, might better serve as a concept to estimate the willingness of a community to designate certain individuals as musicians and support music through various forms of material and cultural approbation.

> The "true" specialist is a social specialist; he must be acknowledged as a musician by the members of the society of which he is a part. This kind of recognition is the ultimate criterion; without it, professionalism would be impossible. Although the individual may regard himself as professional, he is not truly so unless other members of the society scknowledge his claim and accord him the role and status he seeks for himself (Merriam 1964:125).

Professionalism, therefore, exhibits various gradations. It is not a question of being a professional or not being one. Some musicians subsist entirely on the money earned from performance; in some societies the system of reward is sufficiently limited as to prevent any individual musician from living entirely on the basis of musical activities. Professionalism is often a component of other categories of specialization. Instrumental musicians, for example, may receive a specific payment on the basis of their skill. Deviant status may permit a musician to engage in other behaviors that accumulate wealth; in Basongye society, for example, deviant musicians even have greater license to procure goods dishonestly. Despite the claims that professionalism removes the performer from the sanctions of the audience, quite the opposite usually occurs. Even an extreme form of specialization like professionalism requires that the performer understand intimately and observe carefully the existing social norms and the tolerance for change. To do otherwise would effectively terminate professional status.

Most folk musicians are innovative and creative on some level. They may accept or reject change; they may rigidly observe tradition or wantonly violate it. But innovation and creativity do not exist without restrictions. If the folk musician breaches these restrictions, community approbation ceases, and, in some cases society censures. Creativity can be encouraged and yet limited, with the restrictions—the cultural boundaries—symbolizing a metaphorical realm within which creativity can transpire. Accordingly, these boundaries heighten the awareness of both the community and the folk musician of the potential function of creativity in the expression of tradition and the tendency toward change. Creativity, too, serves to juxtapose stability and change and to determine the aesthetic forms both will take. The folk musician's creativity is yet another factor undergirding the dialectic of tradition.

SIX

Folk Music in Non-Western Cultures

> Although folk tunes of different nations differ from one another, and they all differ in certain respects from art melodies, yet they are one and all constructed upon the same fundamental and scientific principles.
>
> Cecil J. Sharp (1965:46)

> Continued study and research into the origins of the folk music of various peoples in many parts of the world revealed that there is a world body—a universal body—of folk music based upon a universal pentatonic (five tone) scale. Interested as I am in the universality of mankind—in the fundamental relationship of all peoples to one another—this idea of a universal body of music intrigued me, and I pursued it along many fascinating paths.
>
> Paul Robeson (1958:123)

> I guess all songs is folksongs, never heard no horse sing 'em.
>
> Attributed to Big Bill Broonzy
> (Keil 1966:38)

A perusal of *The New Grove Dictionary of Music and Musicians* (Sadie 1980) might lead one to the conclusion that most nations of the world have musical repertories with two fundamental subdivisions: art music and folk music. This might not seem an unreasonable way of categorizing music in Austria or Norway, but one wonders in the cases of Mexico and Australia whether the bifurcation is really quite that simple, especially when further examination of the section devoted to Australian folk music reveals such cohabitants as "Aboriginal music," "British and Irish influences," and "Jazz and popular music." Not to be unfair to *The New Grove*, which also employs other approaches to the categorization of national and regional musics, but there can be no doubt that the encyclopedia's editors would claim that folk music is fairly ubiquitous in the world's cultures.

And why not, if we're to believe Paul Robeson or Big Bill Broonzy? The call for universality in music often centers on folk music and its presumed ubiquity. If we're all folk and we all make music, there must be folk music everywhere. But what about those cultures in which such conditions do not widely obtain? What about societies in which music-making carries a stigma? And those in which concepts of music-making are so ambiguous as to exclude most of those activities that would be called music in Europe and North America?

For all its Romantic, Marxian, or plain downhome appeal, the notion of folk music's ubiquity is particularly Western. It derives from sociological strategies that accept the stratification of Western industrial society, but it is applied frequently to societies elsewhere, with or without patterns of stratification akin to those in the West. In many Western models attributing universality, folk music rarely occupies a cultural realm by itself but forms a stratum apart from, yet contiguous with, art, popular, or religious music. This stratum becomes increasingly inappropriate the more non-Western societies fail to stratify as in the West or persist in relatively homogeneous structures. One may or may not be tempted to claim that folk music accordingly becomes more difficult to identify. Perhaps folk music exists only in contradistinction to art music; perhaps the universality envisioned by Paul Robeson would initially require the rise of ideal, unstratified societies throughout the world.

It is not my intent in this chapter to argue for or against the universality of folk music; rather, I examine here some of the contexts of folk music that are characteristic of certain non-Western societies and that may or may not have counterparts in the industrialized West. I take as a premise that there are musical genres and activities identifiable as folk music in non-Western societies, but I do so only with the caveat that these genres and activities may reveal very different ways of thinking about music and culture in these societies. The more one observes different ways of conceptualizing music, the more one is forced to admit that a putative universality of folk music could never lie in the sameness of musical vocabulary or the homogeneity of social stratum. Instead, it is change in folk music that has a wider currency than many theories would hold, and, indeed, it is change in many non-Western societies that empowers folk music to assume widely varying cultural functions.

Whence the Stratification of Folk Music?

The indigenous literature discussing folk music in non-Western societies has often attended times of nascent nationhood. Folk music, whether the isolated subject of this literature or a component in more comprehensive discussions of national culture, appears as a particularly appropriate symbol for past, present, and future. The authors of such literature assert that folk music has long existed and that it embodied a spirit that was now fully manifest in the national aspirations of the people. Thus, it is the moment of most rapid and dramatic change that called for an assessment of the most traditional and timeless quality of folk music.

> In a rapidly changing society such as Ghana where everyone is reaching out for new forms of expression in social life as well as in music, literature and art, the study of the African heritage of "folk music" is of particular importance, for it is in this idiom that African musical values developed over the ages are enshrined (Nketia 1963:1).

This literature rarely discusses folk music by itself. Instead, folk music is compared and contrasted with other forms of cultural expression. Not only does such comparison justify one form of cultural expression in relation to another, but, more important, it serves as a claim to a broadly based national infrastructure. Folk song defines nation in this literature, and it does so by virtue of its role in an extensive model of indigenous stratification. Thus, P. Sambamoorthy's contradistinction of folk and classical music in India might well mirror the contrast of Great Tradition and Little Traditions.

> Under folk music is included all the songs that do not strictly come within the sphere of art music. Classical music is essentially intellectual music and is the music of the *upper ten thousand*. For an appreciation of classical music one needs to know its science. But this is not necessary in the case of folk music. . . . Folk songs help us to discover the real feelings and ideas of a people. They furnish a lot of information of sociological value. Verses are added to or subtracted from as new ideas come in and old ones pass away. The up-to-date inner feelings of a people always find expression in their songs. These songs are a faithful reflection of all popular sentiments and beliefs (Sambamoorthy 1952:141).

The patterns of stratification that one observes in much of the literature concerning folk music in non-Western nations bears marked similarity to the patterns employed by those authors of *New Grove* articles who subscribed to the coexistence of folk and art music. The old accompanies the new; the simple underlies the complex; the local precedes the national (cf. Lu Zhiwei 1984). The question that must concern us here is whether models of stratification ensue from the preexistence of folk music (or art music), or whether the convenience of ascribing stratification leads to the arbitrary description of some musical practices as folk music. When introducing the music of *a nation*, does one necessarily need to accept some genres of folk music and some form of art music? Was there folk music in non-Western cultures before those cultures became nations?

These questions are in part moot because of the paucity of literature concerning the conceptualization of music at the local or regional level in non-Western societies. The literature that does exist, however, suggests that many non-Western societies do have means of distinguishing categories for musical practices and that folk music is expressed by these categories in manifold ways. Concepts of folk music may derive from setting, social function, lineage, literacy, role in the exchange of goods, or urbanization. Most often, concepts result from combinations of these categories and their formation of such dichotomies as rural versus urban. Hiromi Lorraine Sakata, whose research has persistently focused on questions of the concepts that underlie Afghan musical practices, has identified setting as a primary distinction of folk music from other genres (1983:11). The role of certain genres in social exchange may also determine which genres are considered local and which external to the community (Lortat-Jacob 1981:88–90). The interaction of folk and classical music is also not uncommon as a means of expanding dichotomy into stratification (Sambamoorthy 1952:142 and Nketia 1963:1).

Many concepts of folk music—Western and non-Western—stress both what it is and what it is not. They express indigenous understanding of the complexity of musical culture. That complexity necessarily precludes any isolation of folk music as a phenomenon timeless and unchanging. The particular changeability of folk music in a given society thus depends on what dichotomies it demonstrates, what other genres it is in contact with, and what social functions it complements. These may reveal a society with a high degree of stratification or relatively little cultural differentiation. But whatever the form of complexity or change a society manifests, folk music participates in it.

Our Music, Their Music

Common to most societies, ethnic groups, or communities are ways of designating folk music that is their own. A sense of ownership often reflects a sense of boundaries and the musical territory that they enclose, if not also that which they concomitantly exclude. In part, it is this sense of musical domain that accounts for the concept of musical culture so frequently invoked by eth-nomusicologists. Nomenclature may reflect ownership and location; in Af-ghanistan, for example, adjectives commonly denote folk songs by indicating origin in a particular region or among a specific ethnic group, but textual and musical contents remain unspecified in this fashion (Sakata 1983:56). This sense of musical ownership, furthermore, reflects group identity, that is, those pat-terns by which a community distinguishes its own culture and seeks to express that culture.

The constraints that determine which musical styles and genres belong to a society range from the very restricted to the relatively tolerant. Some con-straints function most effectively by exclusion; others result from the interaction of the different styles and genres within a society's musical culture. An aware-ness of musical ownership may be widespread, or it may only characterize particular groups—for example, those who function in some way as specialists. In some societies, music serves as a metaphor for other forms of cultural expres-sion, thereby acquiring other boundaries and enhancing the meanings and values attending ownership. If music and myth interact closely in a particular society, new patterns of ownership frequently emerge as musical practice par-allels the expression of myth or serves even as its source (Basso 1985:245).

There are many ways whereby a society or community can enforce its musical domain. One of the most prevalent means of determining what folk music is "ours" is to contrast it with "theirs." Thus, local or regional music stands in opposition to supraregional or more international music. This opposition may result from different linguistic or musical styles or from social function, which may be more closely integrated into community life. As the binary oppositions signaling "ours" and "theirs" proliferate in a community, the conceptualization and expression of musical proprietorship accordingly increase. In Afghan society such oppositions at many levels—formal and informal, public and private, professional and amateur, male and female, instrumental and unaccompanied—create a conceptual distance between many musical practices and the potential onus of Islamic law (Sakata 1983:19). This conceptual distance is greatest in those practices for which the sense of musical ownership is most acute. Such practices also demonstrate most clearly the characteristics of folk music (ibid.:28 and 33).

As the social structure of a community and its contacts with other commu-nities become more complex, so too do the patterns delineating musical do-minion. In Kaluli society in Papua New Guinea, song composition is dependent on a knowledge of local audiences and nearby geography (Feld 1982:136). The difference between "our" music and "theirs" is therefore based on the Kaluli articulation of a mythical world, with its invisible components, as a metaphor for the visible world the Kaluli inhabit. The creation of song results from the bringing together of the "inside" and "outside" realms of this metaphorical dichotomy (ibid.:166). In societies where cultural pluralism predominates, repertories of "our" music may result from conscious choice or ascription. Immigrant groups often selectively determine those musical genres that will best articulate their identity. As suppressed ethnic groups in the Middle East attempt to stake claims for a political voice, they strive also to identify and foster their folklore and folk music, thus giving their political claims an explicit cultural license. The multiplication of centers for the study of Palestinian folklore on the Israeli-occupied West Bank is one of the clearest examples of the conscious creation and re-creation of a sense of musical and cultural domain (Committee for Palestinian Folklore and Social Research 1986). Folk music in such situations of complex culture contact is far from static but changes rapidly to acquire new patterns of meaning, attributing new musical boundaries to a community as its sense of musical ownership continuously refines the awareness of "our" music and "their" music.

Few musical cultures exist in the world without important roles—sometimes central roles—accorded to outsider musicians. What those roles are may vary tremendously from culture to culture, but commonly the outsider's role is one of enforcing the balance between "their" music and "our" music. The outsider musician is a conduit to another musical repertory, which, by virtue of the outsider's role, becomes an inseparable component of "our" musical culture. The notion of "their" music, then, does not necessarily signal exclusion; rather, it may be the representation of otherness within a community's own folk music. The balance between "our" music and "their" music may indeed be the dialectic binding core to boundary.

Only extreme isolation permits a situation in which indigenous folk music occludes all traces of other musical repertories. Throughout this study I have argued against the retention of isolation as a definition of folk music. In contrast, I view as more significant to a reappraisal of folk music in the modern world the recognition of musical cultures in which the mixture of local and external genres is considerable. Examining the role of the musical professional known as ᶜasheq in effecting the balance of diverse musics in ethnically complex Khorasan in northeastern Iran, Stephen Blum has postulated that the ᶜasheq's success rests primarily on his ability to perform music of indigenous, Kurdish, Turkic, and popular Persian origins (1972:32). The ᶜasheq therefore serves several sectors of Khorasani society. His repertory allows him to move fluidly among the different ethnic and social groups of Khorasan. As an outsider in various venues, the ᶜasheq purveys an art viewed by many groups as an acceptable rapprochement of local concepts of music and Islamic teachings, made possible by the conscious admixture of music with more local associations and that with external connotations (ibid.:42). The coexistence of "our" music and "their" music might well be cause for eliminating such designations, but it also reveals that musical boundaries are constantly shifting within the musical culture of Khorasan, a process of change necessary in a region where Islamic prescripts could potentially negate local practice.

Concepts of musical ownership and foreignness define the boundaries of a musical culture in various ways. The boundaries of a musical culture may be ethnic, and folk song may belong inside or outside because of its language. The distribution of musical skills and specialized media of performance limit genres of folk music to certain groups. Musical genres and even certain pieces may stake out their own musical territories (Ives 1983). This flexibility of boundaries reveals that the determinants of "our" music and "their" music are subject to constant change. In different cultures the boundaries may exist at varying cultural levels and in relation to contrastive folk music genres, thus yielding quite different patterns of musical domain. In many Western cultures, the boundaries are largely the result of national, linguistic, and generic determinants; denoting a folk song as a German ballad in Saxon *Plattdeutsch* exemplifies each of these determinants.

For the folk music of some non-Western cultures, generic and linguistic identification may exhibit a different relevance, and, instead, boundaries may arise because of the particular structure of society. In many Berber communities of the Moroccan High Atlas, for example, a musical boundary falls between the practices of the elderly and the young men of the community, the former exclusively practicing the traditionally communal music, the latter a more specialized music that also bears urban and Arabized influences (Lortat-Jacob 1984:24). The youth of the community therefore transpose the music of the outside into the community, where it functions dialectically with the more conservative repertory, thereby effecting a shift of musical boundaries to the community itself and providing specific directions for change. As change occurs, "our" music and "their" music come increasingly into a coexistence within the same community.

Collectivity, Specialization, and Professionalism

Speculations that folk music is universally practiced inevitably stress the ubiquity of the practitioner and the product—"we're all folks" or "it's all folk music." Rarely, however, does such speculation account for the dynamics of performance: how does transmission take place; under what conditions and at what occasions do all "the folks" sing; how does style of performance relate to community structure; how does community structure make it possible for the entire community or, instead, a select group of specialists to maintain the traditional canon? These are only a few of the questions that arise when the performance and function of folk music are more broadly considered. When considered in relation to many non-Western societies, it is these dynamic aspects of performance that cause claims to universality to founder.

One of the most important corollaries to the dynamics of performance is the degree of musical participation in a community: who performs; who constitutes the audience; whose musical activities designate specialized skills or value-laden roles in the community. In modern Western society, participation in musical activities is highly specialized, especially with regard to music's role as an economic commodity; production and consumption of music both rely on high levels of professionalization. Participation in non-Western cultures demonstrates relatively greater differentiation than in the West, forming three general categories, which, though idealized, describe three very different social roles for folk music. These three categories encompass a range from collective performance to specialization in which music takes part in social exchange to patterns of professionalization not dissimilar from those in Western societies.

Cultures in which many social activities are collective and expressive behavior is to a considerable degree nonliterate are often referred to as tribal. Many studies of folk music examine also the music of highly communal societies (cf. Nettl 1973:1–3 and 125–79), in part because the music of some communal societies, notably African, has become an important component of Western musical genres, and in part because communal musical behavior has long suggested a model, if indeed stereotyped, for the role of folk music in any society. Although comparative studies of societies in which collective music-making predominates are relatively few, it is clear that a single model in which everyone participates in all musical activities grossly oversimplifies the nature of such societies. Indeed, even collective music-making has degrees of specialization and quite distinct roles for different genres of music. Societies in which collective music-making is most intensive are those in which few activities of any kind take place in isolation. Among the Kalapalo of Brazil, for example, the power of music lies in its collective performance and its abilty to embrace all other types of cultural expression in order to generate ritual (Basso 1985:245). In other societies, collective performance and individual music-making may coexist, each dependent on different contexts; such societies are relatively common in West Africa (Nketia 1974:23–24). Some observers even argue that collective music-making is itself but a stage in the gradual abandonment of individual control over music as societies become more complex (Lortat-Jacob 1984:19). The complexity of collective music-making thus varies greatly; it is not merely a matter of all people performing all music.

Specialization, too, takes many forms in non-Western societies. Its incipient stage may be the designation of special venues or times for performance, thereby imputing to music specialized roles in the social space and temporal cycle of the community (Nketia 1974:31 and Lortat-Jacob 1984:19). Communities often sanction specialist-performers, sometimes to reinforce the musical canon and at other times to infuse the canon with some aspects from outside traditions. In some cases, musicians are among the only (or first) specialists in a society that is otherwise extensively communal (Schuyler 1984:91–92; this is a fundamental argument of Jacques Attali, 1985:12–15 and 21–45, in his model of music's position in the political economy of Western culture). Specialization also takes the form of skills—for example, the ability to play a musical instrument—that few others command. But such skills do not in themselves negate the possibility of widespread collective performance (Lortat-Jacob 1981:90). Specialization in many societies results in social exchange, that is, the trading of one form of cultural activity for another so that the web of cultural interaction is complete in itself. Thus, a community may depend on a core of specialized instrumental musicians to accompany many different social occasions, which together represent a cooperative, if not collective, society.

When specialization results in more than social exchange, when remuneration measures audience response, specialized musicians also become professional musicians. Professional performers differ from the simply specialized in yet another way: they maintain considerably more intensive and more frequent contacts outside a single community. In some cases, this may be a result of limited performance opportunities or musical events confined primarily to specific festivals (Lortat-Jacob 1984:19). If performers rely on music for their primary source of income, they must travel to where employment can be located, and they are thereby transformed ipso facto into outsiders (Schuyler 1984:91–92 and Attali 1985:14–15). In many societies, musical professionals bear those traditions that are questionable or proscribed, or, conversely, accorded special value. In general, they extend the social distance between music-maker and music receiver. This social distance, however, need not suspend collective musical performance. More characteristically, new groups form as societies become more complex, creating in the place of overall collectivity sublevels in which these groups spawn new forms of expressive behavior. Complex societies may then come to be characterized by a sort of collective pluralism, replete with new boundaries and new canons of folk music.

The overlap between these idealized forms of society and community is considerable, but it is the interstices that are suggestive of the position of folk music performance in non-Western cultures. Thus, not the purely communal but the mixture of communal with specialization distinguishes folk music in relatively unstratified societies. And in highly complex societies, musical specialization may represent the shrinking of social distance in small groups, just as professionalization of the society as a whole amplifies the gap between musical production and consumption. In these interstices, one observes folk music being created and re-created. Exactly how this happens depends on how a particular society confronts the changes necessitated by greater specialization or the call for social reform entailing more extensive collectivity. If we are to understand folk music in the different contexts of non-Western cultures, it becomes necessary to examine these interstices ethnographically, to determine how they are similar or different from those evident in postmodern Western culture. Pursuing a bit further the problems that inhere in such ethnography, I turn to the musical cultures of the Middle East, first to ask whether one can talk about folk music in Islam at all, and then to suggest some tentative ways of identifying those practices that lend themselves to investigation as folk music.

Folk Music in the Middle East

It is impossible to study any aspect of culture in the Middle East without also considering the impact of Islam. A study of folk music is no exception to this rule. Islam lends historical, cultural, and, to some extent, political unity to the Middle East, and some might claim that Islam ipso facto defines the Middle East. As a religion, Islam is also unified by language, namely Arabic in the Qur'ān; by extension, much religious music bears witness to a unifying linguistic boundary. The sweeping unity of Islam, however, is to some degree theoretical or heuristic, for cultural differences in the Middle East—not to mention political differences—often far outweigh the force of potential unity. To the most rigidly conservative exegetes of Islam, whether defenders or detractors these differences are but momentary diversions that cannot fundamentally alter the ineluctable course of Islam itself (e.g., Hitti 1970).

Islam is not the only source of cultural unity in the Middle East. Other forms of unity, perhaps more deeply embedded, are manifest in several types of cultural expression, music clearly among them. The genres of classical music in the Middle East, including North Africa, Turkey, the Levant, the gulf states, Persian-speaking areas, and much of Central Asia, demonstrate a unity of modal foundation and formal process. At the very least, these musics resemble each other more than they resemble the music of contiguous culture areas outside the Middle East. Again, however, unity is marred by the exceptions characteristic of linguistic and national dialects, and by musical practices that belie the existence of any form of overall cultural unity.

Considered as a whole, folk music in the Middle East—its contexts and its

texts—may serve as evidence for or against claims of cultural unity. If interpreted as a panoply of little traditions, folk music might be counterpoised against
some form of great tradition, indeed one demonstrating cultural unity. But if
its diversity bespeaks a more pervasive differentiation or an intransigent response of regional culture to Islam, then claims to unity break down. These
two positions of folk music in the Middle East rest on two different theories,
one asserting that folk music originates in local practice, the other claiming that
folk music bears witness to the larger cultural system of which it is a part. It
is with considerable uneasiness that one searches for evidence to support both
of these theories in the Middle East.

Islam and music. Complicating the study of music in the Middle East are
the questions of interpretation arising from Islamic attitudes toward music.
These attitudes range from contentions that Islam condemns music outright to
judgments that Islamic writings are at best ambivalent toward its practice. Two
primary literary sources are traditionally used to justify the interpretation of
music's acceptability: the Qur'ān and the many interpretive works concerning
Mohammad's teachings called *ḥadīth* (plural, *aḥādīth*). Neither source is unequivocal in its pronouncements concerning music. The Qur'ān contains *surat*
(chapters; singular, *surah*) that seem to condone activities associated with music,
as well as *surat* cited as evidence that Mohammad condemned music (Farmer
1967:22–24). But even these writings do not address music per se but rather
cultural activities with which music might be associated, such as poetry. Neither
music nor the other arts seem to have greatly concerned the Prophet, at least
as far as his teachings are recorded in the Qur'ān. Moreover, there is relatively
little detailed discussion of the arts by the earliest theologians of Islam (Grabar
1973:18). The early Islamic writings that do include discussions of the arts
seldom offer any doctrine that might be called a theory of aesthetics. In the
aḥādīth, precedence of religious concern results from rather strict principles
of priority that subsequently become the basis for authority, and music has
relatively little precedence (al Faruqi 1985:4). Most early writings referring to
music treat it circumstantially together with pre-Islamic beliefs or social phenomena that Islam does not condone. *Aḥādīth* also originated frequently in
lands conquered during the spread of Islam, and they therefore initially referred
to the cultural activities therein in very specifically didactic ways.

Early Islamic writings are neither theological nor aesthetic in their observations of music. They simply describe a desirable cultural context for Muslim
society and prescribe, rather than proscribe, the most appropriate functions
for music and the other arts within that context. Exegetes estimated as acceptable those genres of music accompanying public festivals, rites of passage,
family celebrations, and the social activities of the smaller community or oc-

cupational groups (Farmer 1967:35 and al Faruqi 1985:8). In a hierarchy of musical activities ranging from musical to nonmusical, such genres most often qualified as nonmusical, thus rendering them legitimate, or ḥalāl (al Faruqi ibid.). It is these genres, moreover, that most closely approximate folk music when interpreted from the standpoint of social function, which is also a criterion of interpretation used by many Islamic legists. Folk music in the early Islamic Middle East, to the extent that it is viewed as a component of other cultural activities, has far less stigma attached to it than many other types of music; relatively speaking, the permissibility of folk music is not attacked in Islamic legal writings.

Both interpretive writings and the continuation of practice contain multifarious views concerning the permissibility of music. If the surfeit of interpretation fails to identify specific types of acceptability, one can identify certain patterns in which some musical practices are relatively less problematic than others. In those settings that draw widespread criticism, music receives few remarks of approbation. Accordingly, there are some settings in which the awareness of Islamic attitudes is very keen, some settings in which indigenous concepts of music reflect only vague recognition of the possibility of stigma. This dichotomy undergirds another contrast in Afghanistan, where urban musicians are far more sensitive to Islamic pronouncements than are rural musicians (Sakata 1983:11).

The boundaries of acceptability. When different settings engender different views, a form of cultural distance tempering musical attitudes arises. Different views also extend to different types of musician. Some musical activities are appropriate to community members, others only to musicians widely recognized as outsiders. The status of outsider distances a setting for performance, both figuratively and literally, from the core of community musical attitudes. The status of outsider may result from a musician's living outside the community itself, which is often the case with Jewish musicians, who have not infrequently constituted the primary performance ensemble in several Muslim societies (cf. Loeb 1982 and Warkov 1986). Sometimes it is because a musician is a specialist that outsider status accrues to him or her; Egyptian epic poets are often labeled as outsiders—for example, as gypsies—whether or not there is any evidence from the poet's lineage to suggest the appropriateness of such a label (Slyomovics in press). Often the musician is called an outsider even when he may have lived much of his life in or near the community where he most frequently performs. In such cases, one might say that cultural distance is employed to supplant the lack of geographic distance, thereby relegating observance or denial of Islamic proscriptions to the cultural realm of the outsider.

Musical terminology throughout the Middle East frames the articulation of distinctions between the acceptable and the questionable. Recitation of the Qur'ān (*qirā'ah*) and the call to prayer (*adhān*) are not musical activities, but genres designated as "reading," one of the literal meanings of *qirā'ah* (al Faruqi 1981b:57–62; cf. al Faruqi 1981a). The role of music in the reading of religious texts is that of enhancing the meaning through clarification. Hence, what to the Western observer sounds like music is unquestionably secondary to matters of textual projection and religious expression. Throughout the Middle East, genres of strictly vocal music are greeted by less disfavor than are genres employing instruments. When the terminology describing local music also connotes folk music, genres of unaccompanied song frequently are subsumed by the terminology.

Instrumental genres, in contrast, often bear terminological witness to a quality of cultural distance. One encounters, for example, the widespread use of the term *mūsīqā* (or *mūsīqi*), which was borrowed from Greek; the term can never apply to *qirā'ah* or *adhān*. Among the Islamic sciences *mūsīqā* occupies the position of "foreign," which serves as yet another level of cultural distancing. Terminological distinctions are used to calibrate cultural distance, as in describing secular music that is strictly vocal as *ghina'* (song), thus stripping it of possible associations with instruments. Historically, the term *mūsīqā* has been applied to musical practices that incorporate instrumental genres into unacceptable settings. Coffeehouse proprietors, for example, traditionally hired musical ensembles, often of considerable size, to attract customers; in such cases, one form of disreputable activity complemented another, generally making for good business (Hattox 1985:106). Lebanese proverbs that address some aspect of music consistently group musicians with less desirable members of Lebanese society, thus projecting music in a negative light (Racy 1985:83). Terminology, practice, setting, folklore: all draw attention to the boundaries of acceptable musical practice.

Folk Music at the Cultural Core; Folk Music at the Boundaries

Responses to Islamic attitudes toward music frequently result in two concepts of folk music and folk musician in the Middle East: the local (or regional) and the professional. The two concepts are clearly not parallel and thus reflect two ways of thinking about music. The first way is most frequently articulated in relation to place, the second in relation to performer. Moreover, the concept of place stands closer to the cultural core of a community, ethnic group, or nation, whereas the concept of professionalism tends to define certain boundaries of acceptability. The first falls within categories deemed legitimate in legal hierarchies of musical genres; the second may, and often does, contain genres that would be judged controversial or even illegitimate (al Faruqi 1985:8). The two concepts coexist within most communities, though the importance of one or the other varies. It is this balance that represents the ways in which cultural core and boundary are mediated. It illustrates, moreover, just how folk music reflects cultural attitudes that are inherent in the community and those that influence the community from without.

The extent to which the two concepts produce a clear bifurcation often depends on the distinctiveness of the community, that is, its cultural distance from the model of unity imputed to Islam. The two concepts are quite clear, for example, in the Berber communities of the High Atlas and Sus regions of Morocco studied by Philip D. Schuyler (1979). He has identified four general types of music, including two secular types that are similar to the two concepts of folk music I have posited here. Village music, *ahwash*, describes local genres. It is performed by local villagers and differentiated according to each village, whose boundaries therefore circumscribe it. *Ahwash* functions for the village as a symbol of village stability and collectivity. The contrastive role of music is fulfilled by *rwais* (reciters), itinerant professional musicians who form small groups, the composition of which is in more or less constant flux. The music of the *rwais* differs dramatically from *ahwash*, for the professional musicians move from village to village and even to other areas of North Africa and occasionally to Europe. Whereas *ahwash* is specifically local music, the songs of the *rwais* make frequent reference to the outside world, functioning even as a sort of chronicle of external news (Schuyler 1984:92). The music of the *rwais*, in contrast to village music, requires great flexibility, which results from the use of small, relatively fixed units that lend themselves to considerable combinatorial freedom (ibid.:93). *Ahwash* and the performance of the *rwais*, therefore, occupy respectively the core and boundaries of Moroccan Berber culture.

Professional musicians may have functioned as mediators of musical change for various types of local music for centuries. In Moroccan Berber communities *rwais* predate mass media, thus making it impossible to associate them specifically with modern processes of de-isolation (ibid.:92). Edward William Lane observed very specific types of professional musicians in early nineteenth-century Egypt, many of which could mediate different cultural attitudes toward music.

> The male professional musicians are called "Alateeyah;" in the singular, "Alatee," which properly signifies "a player upon an instrument;" but they are generally both instrumental and vocal performers. They are people of very dissolute habits; and are regarded as scarcely less disreputable characters than the public dancers. They are, however, hired at most grand entertainments, to amuse the

company; and on these occasions they are usually supplied with brandy, or other spiritous liquors, which they sometimes drink until they can no longer sing, nor strike a chord (Lane 1966:361).

The professional musician may have a variety of social roles that accompany his or her musical activities. One important type of Afghan musician, the *shauqi* (amateur), has an antonymous occupational designation that enables him to engage in a gamut of other activities—from gambling to training animals to patronizing dancing boys and female entertainers—in addition to playing musical instruments as an amateur (Slobin 1976:23). Such associations may serve to diffuse public scrutiny otherwise directed specifically at music-making. Embellishing references to a musician's outsider status may serve also to diffuse public scrutiny by deflecting it away from music-making per se, thus accounting for the relatively common ascription of terms like *ᶜasheq* to professional musicians throughout the Middle East, in Turkish, Arabic, and Persian cultural areas (Reinhard 1975).

If the status of the professional musician serves to redirect the cultural attitudes toward music, where does music—especially those genres more easily identifiable as folk music—lie vis-à-vis core and boundary? The judgment of music within the community in many areas of the Middle East often focuses more on the performer than on the music itself (Rosen 1984:2–3). It is the performer who is or is not associated with questionable social contexts. In some communities even the most dissolute professional musicians may perform a musical genre that enjoys complete community approbation (Slyomovics in press). A certain neutrality thus obtains in some genres, maintaining their centripetal attraction to the core. Similarly, other musical genres appear to be unchanging and encompass a historical validity inseparable from the cultural core. Throughout the Middle East, sung epics, most of which have both wide currency and local variation, usually maintain such a proximity to the core.

Other genres of folk music reflect the outside influences resulting from greater proximity to the boundaries. But with these genres, too, one can note certain aspects of neutrality. Bartók, in his studies of Turkish folk music, found that urban genres often contained unacceptable textual references, which were obfuscated by poetic and musical complexity in order to neutralize the songs for rural consumption (Bartók 1976:207). Numerous processes of change occur in the musical genres at some distance from the community core, but many of these processes alter the genres in such a way that stratification is rendered ineffective as a characteristic of cultural distancing. Improvisatory instrumental practices, such as that called *taqsīm* in many areas of the Middle East, occur in what might be called folk versions. Bartók, as we witness in a letter to Turkish folklorist A. Adnan Saygun, found it exceedingly difficult to reconcile the presence in Turkish folk music of a technique that he assumed was the prerogative of classical musicians.

> You are right if it is a matter of genuine improvisation, then one cannot consider it to be a "folk melody." However, if improvisations of this kind are in vogue among the peasant musicians of the villages, one must collect them, from a folkloristic viewpoint. . . . In your country it is only necessary to check whether the improvisators are truly permanent village residents or are wandering troubadours. In the latter case one one must consider their improvisations with suspicion, with distrust (Bartók 1976:9).

A more relativistic interpretation, would recognize that rural performers shape improvisatory genres to fit local concepts of folk music, thereby drawing the cultural boundaries closer to the community core.

Distance from the cultural core has both predetermined and flexible aspects. Those genres of folk music that have no Islamic stigma attached to them are always close to the core; those genres whose acceptability is a matter of association with other social activities depend on the ability of the performer to mediate the distance between community core and boundary. The professional musician in Muslim society serves to relieve the tensions created by sometimes uncertain attitudes toward music by absorbing the tensions into his own personage and the music he performs. Professional folk musicians thus become agents of active change, diminishing the distance between musical genres at the community core and those near the boundaries. Accordingly, folk music in the Middle East is inevitably a rich amalgam of rural and urban, vocal and instrumental, secular and religious, private and public, timeless and timely. The cultural dialectic from which it emerges—the broadly based stability of Islam and the urgent change necessitated by diverse nations and ethnic groups in contact—is not fundamentally different from many other musical cultures.

Are We Really All Folk?

Examination of folk music in non-Western cultures reveals styles, genres, and concepts both more restricted and more expansive than those generated by Western scholarship to describe folk music in Europe and North America. Neither pentatonic scale nor contradistinction to art music is likely to prove viable as a criterion for universality. If we're all singing folk songs, we still seem ill equipped to discover grounds for stylistic and functional unison. But just as we fail to prove the universality of folk music, we fail also to disprove that folk music is practiced in cultures throughout the world. We fail, furthermore, to show that some of the dynamic functions of folk music in society—ascription of a sense of place, circumscription and circumvention of local mores, division of practice among community and specialist—are noticeably absent in most societies.

The brief overview of folk music in non-Western societies essayed in this chapter identifies contexts and practices characterized by dynamism and change. Folk music was not a component of the monolithic. Even in Muslim societies, with the complex tenets of Islam as potential determinants of all cultural activities, folk music is far more characteristic of the particular and the differentiated than of a broad sweep of cultural unity. Folk music responds to the changing settings of the Middle East and the contrasting communities of its ethnic groups. Stratification clearly exists in some cultures, but its many versions undergo constant flux; folk music and folk musicians constantly mediate social, ethnic, political, and religious change.

As in Europe and North America, folk music exists in non-Western societies as product and process. Scholars have long speculated about the ways in which some products resemble others; this was a premise, for example, of comparative musicology. The similarities these earlier scholars determined, however, were often arbitrary if not artificial. The diversity of folk music in non-Western societies suggests, instead, the profitability of shifting the focus of investigation: from similarities to differences, from products to processes. This redirection of scholarly energy might further reformulate some of the most fundamental questions we ask about folk music; rather than asking what is universal about folk music, we might better ask, Why is there anything universal about folk music?

SEVEN

Folk Music and Canon-Formation: The Creative Dialectic between Text and Context

Kû welat nebe gelo ez kime? (If I have no
country, what am I?)

Temo, barde du Kurdistan (1981)

The dialectical interrelation of text and context has proved throughout this study
to be unusually fruitful for examining musical change and extending the study
of folk music to contemporary settings and non-Western societies. The several
variables that it entails engender considerable flexibility in the identification
and analysis of folk music repertories, freeing us from the constraints of more
conservative approaches that prescribe certain inviolable conditions before
many pieces are admissible as folk music (e.g., purely oral transmission and
anonymous authorship). The cultural contexts of folk music, too, stand freed
from the shackles of hypothetical rural communities or societies whose imposed
stratification bears distinct resemblance to Western models. The dialectic
between text and context is, nevertheless, complex, and its specific applications
to the study of folk music merit further investigation and illustration. One of
the most significant components of this dialectic is the folk music canon, those
repertories and forms of musical behavior constantly shaped by a community
to express its cultural particularity and the characteristics that distinguish it as
a social entity. Because the social basis of a community is continuously in flux,
the folk music canon is always in the process of forming and of responding
creatively to new texts and changing contexts.

Conceived as a dynamic link between text and context, canon-formation
broadens the theoretical framework for the study of folk music in the modern
world and offers numerous practical advantages toward this end. A major prob-

lem confronting the scholar of contemporary folk music is appropriate identification and definition of the community and the musical activity characterizing it. Even for those who prefer to narrow their field to communities that are relatively isolated in the geographic sense, modernization has become an increasingly prevalent influence that is no longer possible to dismiss as irrelevant. Choosing the city as a field, while more honestly dealing with the forces bearing on folk music in the modern world, is also fraught with problems, again intrinsic in the difficulties with which communities and repertories are delimited. Establishing the appropriate links between social and musical frameworks for contemporary folk music has become particularly problematic in the wake of massive and worldwide modernization and urbanization. Positing canon-formation as one approach to conjoining social and musical components within the same framework will not provide a panacea for unraveling all the threads of this complex situation. That framework, however, does offer the theoretical virtue of containing both text and context, thereby including rather than excluding the processes of change that attend modernization.

Folk music canons form as a result of the cultural choices of a community or group. These choices communicate the group's aesthetic decisions—for example, its preference for one medium of musical activity over another. The theoretical basis of the canon thus emphasizes the internal motivations for cultural expression. Its portrayal of external influences stresses that these, too, are choices made by the community, namely the products of decisions to accept or reject (Smith 1984:11). As socially motivated choices, a community's canons bear witness to its values and provide a critical construct for understanding the ways the community sorts out its own musical activities and repertories. The anchoring of folk music canons in community values depends, furthermore, on the community's particular historical awareness, its conceptualization of folk music and musical activities during its past and the way these bear on the present. Folk music canons therefore articulate cultural values both diachronically and synchronically.

The formation of a folk music canon comprises the many facets resulting from the complex interrelation of folk music and community. Implicit in canon-formation are the origins of repertories, the community's indigenous classification system, and the roles played by musicians—and, more important, the location of all these factors in a variety of modern contexts (cf. von Hallberg 1984:1–2 and Altieri 1984:43). To the extent that canon-formation yields theory for the study of folk music, its flexibility enables it to draw from numerous other approaches to the interrelation of text and context. Thus, adaptations of it could easily be compatible with the concepts of ritual process and social drama proposed by Victor Turner (e.g., 1969) or the face-to-face and ludic social formulations of Erving Goffman (e.g., 1967). Even deconstruction, with its insistence on the ability to recontextualize texts, suggests promising theoretical modifications for the complex juxtaposition of different folk music repertories in modern societies (Culler 1982:134–79). The search for links between text and context also fashions for canons the potential of self-criticism, that is, the ability to penetrate the political and ideological abuse of past and present would-be canonizers. This potential is especially important for a reassessment of pseudo canons that have stunted the investigation of many potentially rich fields of folk music research through a misrepresentation of context.

Because canon-formation assumes a flexibility essential to interpreting the inevitable role change plays in the shaping of folk music, its pragmatic advantages are considerable. It employs as a point of departure the description of existing texts and contexts, thereby avoiding the prescription necessitated by a presupposition of links between isolated communities and tamely circumscribed repertories, or between purely oral transmission and restricted formal structure. If there is any prerequisite for this introductory foray into canon-formation and folk music, it is flexibility and the conviction that this flexibility will animate a broadening of the framework for the study of folk music in the modern world.

Folk Music and the Community: Processes of Canon-Formation

The processes of canon-formation result from a community's transformation of cultural values into aesthetic expression. One might say that the general path of these processes is from social context to aesthetic text; the folk music repertory thus becomes genre for the "inscription" of cultural meaning (Ricoeur 1971). Different communities shape and express folk music canons in various ways. Some canons may be defined by their sameness, which might be evident in stylistic and formal coherence. The community accordingly emphasizes centrality by concentrating in its canon those features that it regards as salient to the core of its musical practices. It is through such processes that the community intentionally traditionalizes its culture (Hymes 1975:353–55). Musical behavior throughout the community might therefore invest special meaning in the types of folk music that are widespread and well known in the community.

In contrast, "otherness" may be a factor in the shaping of a folk music canon. The criteria for defining a group's repertory may be exclusive, concentrating less on centralizing certain features than on impeding the influence of those regarded as foreign. This is especially true in the case of subcultures or groups that express their culture through forms of resistance. Music has provided one of the most potent means of expressing the subcultural resistance among contemporary youth groups (Hebdige 1979:126–27). Otherness may also be a source of style and the vehicle for new meaning through the reformulation of a particular group's values by conscious adaptation, rather than encumbrance, of a foreign musical text. The incorporation by Chinese revolutionary groups of Protestant hymn tunes to proclaim resistance to Chinese imperial regimes during the late nineteenth and early twentieth centuries is one of the most remarkable examples of this process of canon-formation. So powerful were the values represented by this musical canon, moreover, that they spurred the gradual expansion of the canon until it formed the basis of *geming gequ,* the "songs for the masses," in the mid-twentieth-century China of Mao Zedong (Wong 1984). While the canon expanded, musical style itself actually consolidated. Such stylistic change is clearly evident in the melody of a song written for the worker's recreational center of the Anyuan road mine project in 1922; popularized during a strike in September of that year, it soon became canonized as an anthem for other strikes (ibid.:118–19). The four-measure and two-measure phrases that frame "Anyuan Lukuang gongren julebu buge" (example 9) clearly give the song a sense of tonality by outlining a dominant to tonic cadence. The second, third, and fourth phrases, however, lack strong tonal implications, and with their use of intervals of an augmented second (transcribed as d-b and a-c) and the further absence of a half step, these phrases employ pentatonic structures characteristic of Chinese melodic styles (ibid.:119).

Many of the processes that we observe when folk music changes are also notable for their undergirding of folk music's canons. Institutionalization, for example, tends to situate folk music in specific activities that cultivate and express the canon. Literacy, both musical and otherwise, intensifies a community's understanding of its canons, effecting new possibilities for centralizing the implicit values. Literacy also makes it possible to establish a more extensive historical continuity and the more formalized tradition that this entails (Kenner 1984:363–64). Patterns of musical specialization result from attitudes toward centrality and musical canon. In this respect, one can make distinctions between active and passive canon-formation, recognizing too the possibility that these may affect textual and contextual realms with slight differences. To be active, canon-formation may require the formulation and acquisition of identifiable skills or musical roles—for example, the ability to play a musical instrument well. In contrast, passive canon-formation may rely more extensively on a community's acceptance of such social reformulation, as the creation of new contexts for the performance of folk music.

Just as modernization has produced more and varied patterns of canon-formation, it has also meant that some of these patterns have become more pervasive as societies develop in certain ways. The emergence of the modern nation-state is one of the primary backdrops for new patterns of canon-formation;

Anyuan Lukuang gongren julebu buge
(Anyuan road mine workers' recreational club song)

Attributed to Liu Shaoqi   1922
Source: Wong 1984:119

bei ren wu ru   ya po de   wei wo   lao   gong,

shi jie xi wo men dang chuang zao, ya po xi wo men dang xiao chu,

chuang-zao shi jie   chu ya po,   tuan jie wo lao   gong.

Translation

We workers are the oppressed people.
We will create a new world,
Eliminate oppression,
Create a new world.
Workers unite.

EXAMPLE 9

so also is the increased cultural heterogeneity that has resulted from the mass movement of population groups. One of the most sweeping responses to these conditions of modernism has been called by Eric Hobsbawm "the invention of tradition" (1983). Hobsbawm uses this concept to account for a specific type of canon-formation—one for which the past is largely fabricated, usually because of the decisions of a few individuals, and continuity with the past has little historical credibility. An invented tradition may centralize an aspect of the past that never really existed, that enjoyed no previous currency whatsoever, much less centrality. Although invented traditions may seem contrived on the surface, they do result from an overt form of canon-formation and the ascription of considerable value to the need to express certain aspects of culture—especially history—in canonical fashion.

Addressing more specifically the generation of cultural traits to fit the emergence of modern nations, Benedict Anderson has proposed the concept "imagined community" (1983). Anderson's study of the canonical foundations of many recent nations is especially instructive because of its attention to the relation of historical time to tradition. To imagine a community requires collapsing the specific consequences of time and place, thereby allowing the appropriation and juxtaposition of previously disparate aspects of culture (ibid.:28–40). Thus, it was necessary for the German Romantics to rely on an imaginary basis for *das Volk* if they were to anthologize folk music in such a way that it could be called *deutsche Volkslieder*. For Nikolai Grundtvig (1783–1872) to establish folk schools in Denmark predicated on the communal functions of the arts (and most notable among the arts, folk music) also required actively imagining a certain type of past and instituting it in nineteenth-century Denmark. Similarly, the intellectual scions of Francis James Child proceeded to imagine communities of ballad singers and social contexts for communal musical activities that had little historical validity. The musical symbols of an imagined community are many: an identifiable corpus of folk song, usually printed for wide distribution; national songs and national anthems; folk songs that spell out the history of the nation in overt and subtle forms; and, in general, the equation of folk music with national music.

It would be only too easy to look disparagingly at the invention and imagination of folk music canons; perhaps I, too, am particularly guilty of berating the persistent promulgators of imaginary Anglo-American ballad traditions for what I consider their unwillingness to abandon a restrictive canon. Clearly, however, the invention and imagination of musical tradition retain many of the characteristics of canon-formation that I have regarded here as particularly valuable. To invent a folk music tradition is certainly to engage in a conscious decision-making process; to implant that tradition through settlement schools derived from Danish folk schools and festivals is to restrict the resulting decisions even more forcefully. And, at least at some level, imagined traditions gain supporters, that is, those who are willing to accept such traditions as representative of a community. Finally, even when a tradition is inappropriately invented, the failure to fit properly is evidenced by flawed seams. That the American South was not a sheltered receptacle of Child ballads has been convincingly argued by David E. Whisnant (1983), and the hegemony of certain song canons in the British Isles is undergoing effective repudiation by a new, critical breed of British folk music scholars (Harker 1985). Moreover, the true diversity of musical styles in the American South is receiving its due attention, producing a scholarship that bears witness to the region's diversity and completing the inchoate canons invented by a previous generation unwilling to accept the change and modernization of the region.

The concept of folk music canon that I introduce in this chapter attempts to interpret the ways in which the community makes its own decisions about musical activity and repertory. Indispensable to this concept is the centrality of the community as a context for musical decisions. This interpretation of canon-formation, however, is only one of several possible approaches. Those theories that are primarily concerned with literary or art history consider canons in a different light, namely by focusing almost exclusively on text. Text-derived canons are notoriously unstable, rising and falling according to the changing contexts of cultural history. Many writers, painters, and composers who enjoyed the highest degree of fame during their lifetimes are now unknown; others, relatively unknown in their day or overshadowed by successors—a Botticelli or a J. S. Bach—experience revival and canonization at the hands of later generations (Kermode 1985:3–31).

How fickle, then, are the processes of canon-formation? Is a canon no more than a flourish of popularity? Or the product of the instincts of those only too well endowed with the ability to second-guess the tastes of their communities? Can texts alone serve as the basis for canons? Or does the isolation of great works actually render canons inchoate, devoid of contextual meaning? The folk music canon clearly exhibits a fundamental difference vis-à-vis the sort of canon forged by scholars for the "fine arts." Without context the folk music canon can only be incomplete. Any revival will founder for lack of a community that can adequately provide a context for its cultivation. The advocates of a purely Anglo-American ballad tradition in the South could attempt to impose texts on the region through settlement schools and folk festivals, but they could not make the region over into their invented context. In contrast, the deliberate creation of *geming gequ* in China properly identified the effective context for mass expression of solidarity, whether in the form of resistance or the voicing of ideological unity, and then adapted the musical and poetic texts to enhance that context (Wong 1984). Canons are therefore inchoate if frozen in time or affixed to a particular place. It is not impossible for folk music to ossify in this way. But interpreting the dialectic between text and context as dynamic necessarily formulates processes of canon-formation that fully admit change and the creativity thereby invested in folk music tradition.

Three Types of Folk Music Canon

Folk music canons are remarkably variable. They may distinguish the musical activities of only a few individuals or the musical activities shared by a vast nation. The variability of folk music canons enables one to examine them in many cultural contexts and to apply them to repertories with quite contrasting processes of change. Canons frequently overlap, but they rarely cease to retain distinguishing characteristics—unless they are in the process of reformulation. In this section I shall look at three patterns of canon formation. A number of criteria could have guided the choice of the three types and concomitant case studies that follow, but contrast in size, which is to say the extensiveness of the community, served as the fundamental criterion. Additionally, other factors exhibit substantial mutability: transmission and origin of repertories differ; the characteristic specialization of musicians is very dissimilar; the relation to other genres of music in the community, though always complex, shapes the folk music very differently. Common to these canons, however, is their vitality and their illumination of the significant role folk music plays in modern contexts.

Size of community affects many factors related to canon-formation. For the members of a community whose canon I have labeled "small-group," it is at least theoretically possible to know each other. Indeed, one of the conscious purposes for forming small-group canons is to create a sense of belonging or to emphasize camaraderie; such camaraderie may be common to a more traditional setting, but it may also provide a social alternative in larger, more urbanized societies. For the members of a community whose canon I have called "mediated," there is often a historical basis for size—for example, residence in a particular geographic region or a shared experience like immigration. One may say, therefore, that the members of such a community share many aspects of culture, but it is physically and geographically impossible to exchange them without mediation. Maintaining the third type, the "imagined canon," is a community that is extremely large and whose boundaries are abstractly positioned. By definition, the imagined canon entails a group whose members may have only tenuous historical connections and who cannot know each other because of the sheer vastness of the community. The boundaries of the community whose corpus of folk music is largely imagined are generally political and frequently equivalent to those of a modern nation-state; in this sense, I stick rather closely to Benedict Anderson's usage of "imagined community" as a paradigm for examining nationalism.

The three types of folk music canon demonstrate three patterns of interrelation of repertory and social structure. For the small group, many pieces in the repertory may articulate specific social activities. This direct interrelation reflects, on one hand, the similarity of the small-group canon to concepts of traditional society, in which folk music is inextricably bound to many cultural activities. On the other hand, establishing a direct interrelation may be a motivation in the formation of small groups in a more urbanized society. Folk music repertory and social structure often have fairly extensive historical connections in the case of mediated canons, although circumstances have intervened to attenuate these connections. Thus, factors like style, rather than specific pieces, may be the most commonly shared aspects of social structure. Because the tradition of an imagined canon may be fabricated, connections between repertory and social structure may be skewed or disjunct. They are not, however, arbitrary, for conscious, carefully calcuated attempts to invent meaningful tradition generated them.

Although the three types can all account for the complex processes of change in modern societies, they do so in somewhat different ways. The small group is relatively independent of modernization. It may be a response to modernization of the larger society, but it may also characterize societies that have undergone rather little modernization themselves. In contrast, a mediated canon depends on modernization to establish its folk music traditions. Modernization provides a means of disseminating folk music, thereby establishing communicative links to different parts of the community. The imagined canon is not so much dependent on modernization as inseparable from it. Insofar as it accompanies broad processes of change such as nationalism, the formation of an imagined canon tends to be a more recent historical phenomenon.

Musical activities, as well as the stress placed on them by the community, differ according to their canonical basis. One might envision these activities heuristically forming a continuum based on the size of the group characterized by a particular folk music. At one end, the small group concentrates on rather specific practices, consolidating and codifying them in a concise repertory. At the other end, an imagined canon may form out of disparate musical practices, drawn from diverse repertories, genres, and social functions. The process of imagining also consolidates these practices, although it is not until folk music traditions are juxtaposed by the same organizations that they crystallize sufficiently to produce a concise repertory. The small-group canon thus has rather specific, contained sources, whereas the imagined canon requires a musical basis that admits diversity.

The small-group canon: Folk music as a basis for German social organization, 1870 to World War I. The small-group canon is found in many social settings. It can be an appropriate description of tribal societies and many forms of traditional society. In the small group, folk music is an element of some shared activities; many members of the group know at least a representative sample of the group's shared repertory. These are conditions under which oral transmission may predominate and the tradition itself may demonstrate relatively little change. Its more traditional bases notwithstanding, the small-group canon also has modern contexts that enhance its value as a critical category. Ernst Klusen, arguing from similar reasoning, has even gone so far as to insist that the small group is the only truly valid category in which to place modern folk music, or rather what he prefers to call *Gruppenlieder*, or group songs (1986). In essence, the small group is a buttress of continued differentiation within modernized societies. Thus, its canon may well emerge as a response to modernization and as a means of emphasizing more intimate cultural expression against a backdrop perceived as homogeneous. This form of response makes the small-group canon especially instructive as a model for studying the persistence of folk music in the wake of modernization.

The proliferation of German folk song societies was in many ways coeval with the rise of German nationalism and the industrialization of German society in the first half of the nineteenth century. Just as German nationalism benefited from the centralization of German culture afforded by a standardized literary language and its inculcation through such institutions as the universities, standardized corpora of German *Volkslieder* gained increasing acceptance. Already at the beginning of the century, choruses, especially men's choruses whose members came from the rising middle class, had established themselves as bastions of folk song. The collection and publication of folk songs became legitimate professional engagements at the fringes of the music academy, and by mid-century several folk music scholars had acquired considerable renown in Germany and in German-speaking areas elsewhere. The most famous of these folk music professionals was Ludwig Erk (1807–83), who in his lifetime founded and directed several choruses, published 130 editions of folk songs, collected some 20,000 versions of German folk songs, and arranged many of them in versions that have remained standard until the present (Salmen 1954 and Gundlach 1969). Erk's labors were the culmination of a movement that began with Herder's pronouncements about the *Volk* and its music, and the subsequent refocusing of these speculations to apply specifically to the German people. In every way possible, modernization undergirded this movement, whether through the printing of songbooks or the implanting of transportation networks that drew together singing societies from far-flung areas for massive singing festivals. German folk music scholarship also benefited from the broad aims of the movement, so that by the beginning of the twentieth century such archivist-collectors as John Meier (1864–1953), who founded the *Deutsches Volkslied-archiv* at Freiburg in 1914, were directing their efforts toward the systematic study and analysis of German folk music.

Around 1871, the date of the political unification of Germany, modernization was animating a response that led specifically to the formation of a canon: the adaptation of *Volkslieder* to suit the needs of small groups. The small groups formed for a variety of reasons, but their names and their repertories generally showed concern for local identification and common occupations. Some of the small groups reflected broader patterns of organization; *Turnvereine* (sporting organizations) that fostered a singing society, for example, were a common feature of most urban centers, although they were not always formalized as participants in nationwide leagues. Many of these small singing societies had limited scopes, and some of them could hardly have had more than a handful of members (Schwab 1973:892–98). Certain groups—for example, such minorities as Jewish organizations—formed singing societies for the first time during this period (Bohlman 1984a:111–65).

If there was a unifying aspect to this counter-movement, it was the urge to formulate musical activities on the basis of the small group. The choice of new repertory for the emergent small group further reflected the concern for forming a canon that expressed a desire for differentiation. The point of departure for most small-group songbooks was the more general corpus of German folk song. Well-known songs were extracted from this corpus, usually to create a sense of familiarity; often, the best-known melodies were used but given new texts specific to the group. When songbooks appeared in multiple editions during this period, they usually bore witness to a historical pattern in which sections with songs for the small group expanded, while the general sections (*allgemeine Lieder*) shrank, eventually serving only ancillary ends.

Aspects of mediation and imagination were present in this counter-movement, but they, too, undergirded the formation of the small-group canon. Mediation appeared as a component of the printing process, which enabled the differentiation of various canons to take place rapidly. To the extent that invention did characterize the formation of some traditions, it seems to have reflected not a yearning for undue historical continuity but rather the immediacy and efficacy of joining together in song. This moment in the history of German folk music was, therefore, one in which *das Volk* was actualized by the group. This reification had some significant social ramifications, notably the ability of many groups to break down socioeconomic divisions (Schwab 1973:891). Moreover, the reification acquired a very specific aesthetic voice: the folk songs in each group's songbook. The group, then, had become the canonical vessel—the molding force enclosing the canon—for certain significant subgenres of German folk song, thereby encouraging a process of diversification against the growing nationalism of Wilhelminian Germany.

The mediated canon: Ethnic old-time music in the Upper Midwest. The mediated canon characteristically draws from several social bases and often cuts across several types of community. In short, it often exemplifies pluralism. Youth subcultures, which might well formulate their musical activities as a mediated canon, often exist as regional or socioeconomic amalgams. In modern contexts, mediated canons may reflect specific confrontations with a mainstream culture, whether or not the culture is homogeneous. The term *mediated* is especially descriptive of this sort of canon because the coherence of musical style it contains inevitably benefits from channels of communication and the distribution of mass-produced forms of music. Without such communication and distribution it would be considerably more difficult to redefine and conflate the diverse musical components of the mediated canon. Mediated canons often characterize groups that are in the process of transition from small to large communities. Thus, a mediated musical style may forge a diverse complement of cultural differences into a normative style that allows a degree of cultural sharing and a more intensive drawing of cultural boundaries. The resulting tradition retains elements of the old while admitting the new in patterns consistent with underlying pluralism.

The folk music of the Upper Midwest has consistently witnessed the formation of mediated canons during the region's roughly 150 years of cultural pluralism. Radio stations, record shops, dance halls, and taverns throughout the region have failed to relinquish a penchant for ethnic musical styles, even though individual concentrations of immigrant-group settlement long ago yielded to the influx of diverse groups and the inevitable cultural cross-influences that result. Ethnic old-time music bears witness to the confluence of diverse components. Diversity, however, has become a basis for a unity that is distinguished by the contrast of its canon with styles in the mainstream. Ethnicity, while it tempers musical style, does not stultify it. Some musicians may freely tap the styles that constitute the mainstream but then select those elements that enhance the particularity of ethnic musical style.

External and internal aspects of musical style often demonstrate different processes of change. The external aspects, often originating in the changing styles of the mainstream, may have a more ephemeral existence in ethnic old-time music; in the 1930s and 1940s, big-band jazz was relatively important as an external influence but has been almost completely supplanted by country-western music during more recent decades. Some styles, perhaps influenced by a few prominent musicians, have been very selective, even idiosyncratic, in their responses to external styles. James P. Leary has documented the influence of the Hawaiian guitar in several ethnic old-time substyles in northern Wisconsin and traced it to a brief but flourishing trade in the guitars during the 1920s (Leary 1986a and b). LeRoy Larson, probably the most significant force in the revival of Scandinavian old-time music in western Wisconsin and Minnesota, is a masterful banjo player, thus making it natural for him to incorporate the banjo into many Scandinavian folk dances, occasionally with a nostalgic parenthesis from Dixieland (cf. Larson 1974 and Minnesota Scandinavian Ensemble 1976). Stylistic elements that more overtly draw attention to ethnicity change more slowly. Dance tunes usually retain a formal integrity; ensemble structures, subject to differing degrees of alteration, rarely abandon all instruments that have particular ethnic symbolism. The visibility and audibility of the boundaries between ethnic and mainstream musical elements are essential for the formation of ethnic old-time style and repertory.

Centrality for ethnic old-time music in the Upper Midwest often rests in questions of style especially insofar as style stems from the organization of musical life. Fundamental parameters of style can be identified in both texts and contexts related to dancing. Contexts for dancing exist in most of the predominant ethnic communities of the region in social and fraternal organizations, ethnic and general holidays and a rather dense concentration of taverns (cf. Leary 1982). The dancing ensemble and its instrumentarium have a framework of standardization, within which variation observes fairly specific ethnic lines—for example, the Slovenian-American predilection for button-box accordions and the prevalence of concertinas in some Polish- and German-American areas (cf. Keil 1982:34–42). Dance styles provide myriad opportunities to vary and differentiate the style and content of old-time repertories. Musicians render well-known tunes, ethnic or from the popular mainstream, with identifiable dialects: Slovenian-American style displays virtuosity; Bohemian-American emphasizes the melody; Polish-American stresses metric contrasts. The identifiability of these dialects notwithstanding, they retain a malleability that lends itself to a pluralistic culture by making it possible for skillful musicians to adapt them to a wide range of repertories.

Mediation of ethnic old-time music has assumed numerous and complex forms. Small and specialized companies currently constitute the core for recorded technology; for the most part, ensembles pay these companies to cut records for them and then assume responsibility for distribution. During the heyday of ethnic recording in the United States (ca. 1920–50), the major recording companies, including Columbia and RCA Victor, issued extensive ethnic lists, and the Upper Midwest provided an important constituency, especially for the recordings of Central and Northern European ethnic music (Gronow 1982). Records produced stars—Frankie Yankovich for Slovenian music, Li'l Wally (Walter Jagiello) for Polish polka style, Hans Wilfahrt (Whoopie John) among German communities—and these stars became models for the consolidation of style. Further refinement of style also followed specific directions as the result of mediation. Concertina players, a subgroup of German-American old-time musicians, now rely on an infrastructure of teaching methods, specialized recordings, concertina clubs, networks for the sale and distribution of instruments, and the symbolic elevation of their art proffered by the Concertina Hall of Fame. The specificity of these mediated components continues to underscore ethnic associations while preventing them from being exclusive. Instead, the stylistic complexity of ethnic old-time music is shared by ethnic groups throughout the Upper Midwest and is a means whereby the canon of folk music continuously serves to nurture an awareness of the cultural processes, both past and present, that shape the region.

The imagined canon: The creation of Israeli national folk music. Necessarily a product of modernism, the imagined canon contains seemingly disparate parts that often form what Lévi-Strauss has called *bricolage*, an assemblage of parts that only together constitute a whole (Lévi-Strauss 1966:1–33). *Bricolage* may be carefully contrived, or it may coalesce more or less randomly. Viewed separately, the components of this cultural system do not suggest the particular role they play in relation to other components. Thus, folk songs often have a quite different function before being adapted for purposes of an imagined canon. The *hora*, which has both official and unofficial sanction as an Israeli national dance, originated in southeastern Europe. Israeli folk dance canonizers co-opted the dance for many reasons, probably least of which was that some early immigrants were acquainted with it. Whether because of its relatively simple structure, which lends itself to quick learning and elaboration, or because of its circular motion and linking of dancers, which evoke the egalitarianism that the early settlers hoped would nourish the new country (Kadman 1968:3), the *hora* entered the imagined canon of Israeli folk traditions virtually unimpeded. Further historical justification was unnecessary.

The *bricolage* of the imagined canon is, in fact, quite independent of history; in some cases, it even requires that history be quietly ignored so that continuity with an imagined past appear unchallengeable. In the context of modernism, however, the impetus to challenge the juxtaposition of seemingly disparate parts is considerably less. Modernism in both the sciences and the arts has rendered *bricolage* normative. Developments in physics in the present century, from quantum physics to proposed new models of multidimensionality in nature, have their parallels in cubism and the collage of narrative references in *Ulysses* (cf. Kenner 1984:369 and Geertz 1983:21). Nationalism, the expression of which proliferates at an ever-increasing tempo, has benefited from this modernist tendency to create cultural canons by collapsing and then conflating previous traditions (Anderson 1983).

Folk music might at first seem an unlikely candidate for the formation of imagined canons, but the frequency of its employment as a national symbol proves otherwise. Those engaged in the formation of an imagined canon of folk music either overlook the absence of continuous and related traditions or simply invent them and then justify their relatedness on the basis of a history that somehow should have been the case, employing a line of argument like the following proviso for Israeli folk music: "Historical conditions precluded the organic evolution of folk music of a strongly defined, national character" (Boehm 1971:column 669). And so the imagined canon has become one of the most powerful and pervasive contexts for folk music.

Like many aspects of modern Israeli nationalism, Israeli folk music is largely the creation of the twentieth century. Even though much of the language used to celebrate Israeli folk music differs not at all from that identifying other folk musics, the circumstances that brought the folk music repertory into being are well known to the shapers and guardians of this canon. For many Israelis writing about their folk music, it seems not the least bit incongruous to note—even on the same page—that Israeli folk music has "tunes whose words and music are fundamentally connected with the land of Israel and its people" and that "with the exception of a few tunes composed by the earliest settlers . . . the era of Israeli folk music began with the arrival in Israel of Joel Engel in 1924" (Keren 1980:55).

To a large extent, the formation of an imagined canon of Israeli folk music was inevitable. Even when the initial groups of settlers arrived in Palestine at the end of the nineteenth century, they represented diverse countries of origin. They shared few aspects of a common folk music heritage; their common national heritage, voiced as diaspora from the ancient land of Israel almost two millennia previous to the modern return, was shaded with obviously romantic hues. At the time of early settlement, there were significant efforts to collect and study Jewish folk music within European communities. The Society for Jewish Folk Song, founded in St. Petersburg in 1908, engaged in major efforts to study the folk music of Eastern European communities (Brod 1976:23); Central European Jews, though less systematic than the St. Petersburg society, began to investigate folk music traditions more rigorously and to publish anthologies from diverse sources (Bohlman 1984a:111–63).

The creation of an Israeli national folk music was first the prerogative of Russian immigrant musicians, the most important of whom, Joel Engel, had been intimately involved with the St. Petersburg society from its inception. The "composers" of Israeli folk song turned to a variety of source materials that they deemed appropriate to their nationalist and ideological ends. Yiddish folk song was an important model; Abraham Zvi Idelsohn's ten-volume *Hebräisch-orientalischer Melodienschatz* (Thesaurus of Hebrew Oriental Melodies) gathered traditional folk tunes from Jewish communities in North Africa and the Middle East (1914–32), and German folk song collections became the basis for publications in Palestine subsequent to the transfer of publishing concerns from Germany in the 1930s. More abstract were the qualities of musical repertories practiced by the Arabic communities already resident in Palestine, but nevertheless inseparable from a Levantine soundscape. The new folk songs forged an imaginary unity, intended to draw different immigrant groups together. Many lent themselves to choral arrangement or performance in such new cultural settings of the country as the kibbutzim. The musical structure of the folk music freely combined new and old, real and imagined. Biblical cantillation guided the setting of Hebrew, even though the Hebrew of the folk songs was itself quite modern. Arabic *maqāmāt*, in contrast, appeared in a variety of forms, albeit far more commonly as quasi-medieval church modes than as a form drawn from Arabic music theory and practice (Cohen and Shiloah 1985:202–3). Other musical activities undergirded and inseminated the new folk music tradition. Many composers of art music, for example, turned toward a style loosely identified as Eastern Mediterraneanism and intentionally imbued this style with traits similar to those in the new folk music; indeed, many composers of art music participated also in the composition of folk music, thereby suggesting that the musical font of emergent nationalism really served all genres of music.

The formation of an imagined canon of folk music continued to provide a model for musical activity through consecutive waves of immigrants. Whereas the canon was of diminished importance to European immigrants after about 1950, immigrants from North Africa and the Middle East turned to it as a means of establishing a foothold in musical nationalism during the 1960s and early 1970s (ibid.:204–5). In this sense, the imagined canon is inseparable from the processes of modern nation-building. Subscribing to the formation of the folk music canon has provided for immigrants to Israel a way of claiming a common cultural core with other immigrants or longtime residents of the country. If, indeed, the canon's continuity with the past is spurious, the continuity it lends to a national agenda in the present is not. Even more remarkable in the case of Israel (but surely in other nations that I might also have examined) is the exemplary role that folk music played in the consolidation of a larger cultural canon. For a community of immigrants, the imagined canon of folk music was a conduit to a common language and a cultural activity in which all could participate: the new folk music was by definition one aspect of a way of life meant to be shared. Unquestionably, embracing the new folk music canon required a leap of cultural faith, but it was a leap many were motivated to make. Though Israeli folk music is incompletely formed as a canon and fundamentally dependent on a diverse community's willingness to juxtapose an imagined past and a rapidly changing present, it relies on a centripetalizing attraction of folk music style and repertory toward a common, pluralistic cultural core, however imagined this core may continue to be.

Folk Music, Canon-Formation, and Critical Folkloristics

The three case studies in the previous section represent three different critical frameworks for the study of folk music. The repertories had contrasting functions; folk music style was not only expressed differently, but it exhibited a wide range of meaning and symbolism for the three communities; the social bases ranged from relatively small to rather large; even the ways in which folk music originated varied considerably and reflected different degrees of tolerance for authenticity, the roles of individual musicians, and the relative dissolution of genre stratification. And yet each of the communities in these three case studies was consciously concerned with the potential of folk music to articulate essential aesthetic concepts and cultural values. Their relative degrees of modernization, urbanization, and political or ideological complexity not-withstanding, these three communities consciously identified and fostered folk music as a genre of expressive behavior with expansive, yet luminous, symbolic meaning.

The folk music canons characterizing these three communities were quite different. In no case did the canon depend on a preexisting community with primordial roots or procrustean cultural boundaries; quite the contrary, each of the canons formed during a period of cultural ferment. Change, however, was not incompatible with the consideration of folk music within this framework because the focus was on the dialectic between context and text, which by definition resolves through change. The centrality of certain folk music texts was not a matter of rural or urban contexts; both were complex and both re-sponded to modernization. The choice of repertory—whether centralized by specific polka styles or created to symbolize the rapid ingathering of diverse immigrant groups—clearly differentiated the community and distinguished it from others. The folk music canon, as a measure of these choices to centralize a repertory as a conscious response to the need for cultural identification, is therefore independent of historical patterns in North America or class structure in Europe. Instead, it aims to identify quite different dialectical interactions—constantly changing and changeable—that provide a framework for understand-ing the virtually infinite range of musical activities that constitute the genre folk music. Examining the ways whereby different canons of folk music form is thus one means of critically situating the genre as text and context in the traditional past, the modern world, and the diverse cultures of non-Western societies.

EIGHT

Folk Music in the Modern World

(Even the most perfect reproduction of a
work of art is lacking in one element: its
presence in time and space, its unique existence at the place where it happens to be.)
This unique existence of the work of art determined the history to which it was subject
throughout the time of its existence.

Walter Benjamin (1969:220)

Time is the substance I am made of. Time
is a river which sweeps me along, but I am
the river; it is a tiger which destroys me, but
I am the tiger; it is a fire which consumes
me, but I am the fire.

Jorge Luis Borges (1964:234)

In some measure and a variety of ways, the
old music has been brought back.

Bruno Nettl (1985:162)

Few visitors to the marketplace of a city in the Middle East can help but find
the sheer quantity and diversity of its musical activity staggering. Layered in
a seemingly cacophonous din at times, the music of the bazaar has a remarkable
order of its own, an order that observes the interplay of geography and the
web of streets and shops in the bazaar itself, as well as the passing hours of the
day and the passing days of the year. Articulating this order are clearly traditional elements: the call to prayer (*adhān*) five times daily, and the traditional
musical roles relegated to ethnic minorities or to musical specialists and professionals. Juxtaposed with the traditional is a different type of musical activity:
the modern. Radios blare; shop owners hawk cassettes of popular singers
based in Cairo, Paris, or Los Angeles; the latest sound-system technology is

on sale everywhere. The old and the new exist side by side, sometimes conflicting but more often coexisting in unpredictable ways, as by the virtually total replacement of the *mu'adhdhin* (one who calls to prayer) with tape-recorded prayers broadcast from minarets. The modern, rather than destroying the old order, has participated in the forging of a new order. Indeed, modern components seem no less compatible with that order than do traditional components.

The musical *bricolage* of the Middle Eastern bazaar is a suggestive metaphor for folk music in the modern world. The bazaar is an amalgam of many musics, styles, and social contexts. Diverse genres of music—religious, popular, folk, and classical—are abundantly in evidence, but almost never in such marked isolation that the stylistic boundaries remain unblurred. The venues for musical performance, too, are manifold, yet sometimes difficult to define and locate precisely. More often, stages exhibit the large measure of flexibility necessary to accommodate shifting audiences and musical tastes. Performers, too, recognize that the bazaar is a setting in which diverse musics are marketed. The most successful know that there is a time and place for the traditional, just as there is an audience more receptive to the innovative. Locating audiences and negotiating musical styles and messages accordingly are matters of survival in the marketplace.

The bazaar also provides the setting in which the juxtaposition of cultural differences is at its most extreme in the Middle East. Ethnicity is an extremely complicated affair. Not only does the more or less sedentary population of the bazaar reflect ethnic diversity, especially if related to the specialization of professions, but the movement of buyers and traders into and out of the market results from exceptionally fluid patterns of pluralism. Ethnic minorities commingle and interact. There are many reasons for villagers with different ethnic backgrounds to gather in the urban bazaar: trade, religious festivals or saints' days, young people seeking jobs in the city. Whatever the reasons for gathering, the bazaar is a crucible for the shaping of new groups predicated on the complex cultural offerings of the market. Social outsiders may thus become insiders, if only within the subsociety of the bazaar. Professional musicians, some undoubtedly scorned elsewhere in the local Muslim culture, are essential to the musical life of the marketplace. Some rules of musical behavior may be violable, but new codes specific to the bazaar arise to ensure the basic order of its musical subcultures.

Modernity pervades the musical life of the bazaar. The affordability of many electronic media has exerted an especially profound effect on music. Not only are recording cassettes convenient and inexpensive to transport from the warehouses of major recording companies; they also lend themselves to rapid copying in large numbers and to piracy, both of which are evident in the thousands of cassettes representing scores of musical styles that almost any tape vendor has to offer. The electronic media constitute, furthermore, a conduit to the outside, to other parts of the Middle East but also to international styles. The outside is easily reached by tuning a radio to such international bands as the BBC World Service with its variety of musical styles ranging from Celtic folk music to country-western. Modernization also has less obvious manifestations in the bazaar. It is likely that one can find shops that sell sheet music or books designed to help the beginner learn to play a musical instrument; techniques of mass production, too, assist in the manufacture of traditional instruments.

Two other factors are intrinsic to this metaphor for folk music in the modern world. First, the bazaar is an urban institution. It is a part of the city; to many of those who use it, the bazaar is synonymous with the city, for it represents the sum total of their interaction with the city. The juxtaposition of subcultures that is so concentrated in the bazaar is a quality of every city. Second, the bazaar is a market. Like other products, music in the bazaar is a commodity. It is bought and sold. Musicians are often professionals, some of whom support themselves entirely by performing in the diverse venues afforded by the market. No musical genre remains immune from its potential sale value. It is just as easy to buy complete cassette recordings of the annual cycle of recitation from the Qur'ān as it is to buy tapes of semiclassical music performed by a studio ensemble. Each genre, in fact, has its star performers, whose lives are well known to the consumer.

The bazaar, in effect, collapses time and space. It is for this reason that it epitomizes so completely the cultural and temporal contexts of modernity (Anderson 1983:28–31). The same collapsing of time and space empowers the bazaar to serve as a metaphor for folk music in the modern world. The old and the new, the traditional and the popular, occur together, simultaneously; they exhibit no correlation of cause and effect and no path of evolutionary change; external chronology cannot properly account for their existence. Musical style and repertory, therefore, need not be tied to a particular time and place. Accordingly, the musical life of the bazaar continues to allow diverse—one could say disparate—musical behavior and repertories that persist because of their relation to each other and the context of the urban marketplace. They may continue as subcultures, but not as subcultures dependent on some form of isolation.

The bazaar illustrates the collapse of time and space from yet another perspective that will illumine our consideration of modern folk music, while introducing a sort of contradiction to that consideration. The cultural simultaneity that obtains in the marketplace is not a recent phenomenon; one might even go so far as to say that it is timeless. Marketplaces, whether in the pre-Islamic

Middle East, medieval Europe, or the nineteenth-century American Midwest have by definition been a locus for diversity. Sufficient evidence exists to suggest that musical activities were relatively abundant in all of these settings, as was that process I have been calling modernization; some of this evidence we know because it takes on a life of its own—for example, in the medieval minstrel fair and the contemporary fiddling contest. The musical culture of the bazaar, with its history of millennia, is therefore not an exclusive case but a reminder that music has always faced modernization. Thus, to study folk music in the modern world is not to specify only an aspect of music in the twentieth century; it is to examine a complex cultural context that has long shaped folk music and certainly will continue to do so. It is, furthermore, to accept the timelessness of that context.

Folk music in the modern world, like the metaphor I have suggested here, has shed any cloak, real or imagined, of isolation. No community experiences only its "own" folk music, whether its external experiences are by its own volition or not. Those settings in which folk music is most actively nurtured—the folk festival, for example—are also those in which the juxtaposition of style and ethnic group are most dramatic, reifying what must be considered a musical marketplace. And yet, the modernization of folk music is a vital process. Far from homogenizing folk music style, modernization emphasizes diversity by bringing it together and concentrating it. By collapsing time and space, modernization encourages new ways of looking at older styles and different repertories and sets the stage for revival and revitalization. Modernization thus creates a bazaar for the confluence of musical repertories and the exchange of musical concepts, and it creates the choice of an appropriate technology to give these repertories and concepts a new voice.

Modernization and Urbanization

Folk music in the modern world undergoes many processes of change, but two large processes—modernization and urbanization—dominate and influence many of the other processes. By portraying the influences of modernization and urbanization rather expansively, I do not mean to contradict studies of musical change that have attributed broad influences to other processes, notably Westernization, which Bruno Nettl couples with modernization in accounting for the massive impact of the West on music throughout the world during the twentieth century (Nettl 1978 and 1985; cf. Kartomi 1981, and Shiloah and Cohen 1983; for models that apply to different forms of expressive behavior, see Levy 1966, vol. 1, and Peacock 1968:217–33). Rather, I am focusing my consideration empirically on the genre of folk music. Quite simply, modernization and urbanization impinge more directly and profoundly on folk music than do many other inclusive processes of change; moreover, most of the changes that folk music undergoes in the modern world can be measured as degrees of modernization and urbanization.

That the two processes overlap is obvious. Urbanization has never been as extreme and rapid as it has been throughout the world in the twentieth century. We observe the ways in which the two processes overlap in the role played by the radio in many rural areas. The radio clearly exemplifies modernized technology, but it mediates a cultural product that is urbanized: the mass or popular music generated in the city. The two processes, nevertheless, frequently influence different aspects of folk music. Modernization often affects most directly the musical and structural aspects of folk music, by altering the way in which oral transmission occurs, for example, or by providing a technology that refashions the role of the performer. Urbanization, in contrast, more directly affects the social aspects of folk music, by supplanting the isolated rural community in which most individuals share in the expressive culture. Still, these aspects rarely change in isolation from each other; instead, they tend to exhibit similar responses to many of the same conditions, further suggesting the efficacy of comparing and contrasting modernization and urbanization as broadly significant processes of change.

Many of the musical changes effected by modernization are external and obvious. The instrumentarium of the folk musician expands, admitting new instruments while rendering others obsolete. There are also deeper transformations of the instrumentarium, including the mass production and reproduction of instruments that were previously handcrafted and personalized. Learning to play musical instruments is also streamlined by the creation of "teaching methods" or the mimicking of style and repertory from records, thereby weakening and replacing certain structures of specialized transmission in the community. Technology is the most obvious type of modernization. Technology provides a means of exposing oneself easily to unlimited quantities of repertories and doing so in a neutral fashion. Thus, each repertory broadcast on the radio has the same social context as every other repertory, with the need to make specific value and social judgments stripped away by the technological medium. Technology creates new audiences, and, when mass-produced like the early phonographs in rural America, it does so inexpensively (Spottswood 1982:63). Radio, records, and tapes reach individuals who would otherwise not participate in the musical life of a community (Wallis and Malm 1984:2–3 and 11–14). One form of passivity may replace another, but passivity, nonetheless, acquires a much broader base. Kenneth S. Goldstein has argued that technological advances have always presaged folk music revivals (1982:3–4). Technology need not destroy the more traditional settings; microphones may intensify the involvement of a community in its musical life by multiplying the number of settings in which folk musicians perform, perhaps freeing ethnic musicians from the confines of a church basement but not necessarily abrogating the external boundaries of the community.

Modernization also enables the juxtaposition of musical and structural aspects, thereby collapsing their temporal and historical specificity. Radio is an expressive medium in which juxtaposition is by definition constant. The record shop markets juxtaposed styles and repertories in complex ways. Not only does the record shop provide a venue for the gathering of vastly different musics, each with its own bin and classification system, but its basic artifact, the single record, intentionally mixes styles and repertories, dialects and genres, to bear witness to the sheer virtuosity of its performers and to broaden its aesthetic appeal—in other words, to make it more effective as a marketing device.

The impact of modernization on folk musicians is sweeping. Modernization creates the notion of a stage as a social space reserved for the performance of music (Neuman 1976:2). The stage imposes a distance between the performer and the audience, which at least momentarily is the rest of the community. The stage has also become very specialized, thus a signifier of the complexity of folk music in the modern world: the festival stage signifies one kind of audience; the coffeehouse mike another; the recording studio still another (Paulin 1980:12–13). Modernization has transformed the ways in which one can become a folk musician, either eliminating traditional patterns of learning or making them ineffective as paths to success according to the diverse extracommunity criteria for success. Virtuosity, to some degree always a measure of the instrumentalist's specialization, has the additional virtue of increasing marketability within many folk music subgenres. Fiddling contests and the sometimes frenetic tempi of bluegrass are only two ways in which the criteria for virtuosity are measured and codified. Technology may further expand the limits of virtuosity by its penchant for juxtaposition, as when recording engineers edit out the rough spots from a performance or patch together the best parts of several performances, thereby transforming the illusion of flawless virtuosity into an ideal.

Urbanization has special bearing in the reconsideration of folk music because of the long-standing role ruralness has played in the definition of the genre. The ubiquity and complexity of urbanization call in question the validity of discussing folk music within a community or social sphere that is geographically, physically, or technologically rural. As urban areas have expanded, ruralness as defined by isolation has become increasingly fictional to the point of being meaningless. Urbanization now affects profoundly even those areas that are not metropolitan centers. Not just technology but fairly constant migration to and from urban centers ensures more or less constant contact with the city.

Urbanization topples one of the most sacred tenets of folk music theory: the distinction between rural and urban. Accordingly, new groups and social divisions have come to characterize folk music, making it necessary to state new tenets that admit the impact of the city on folk music. The interaction of urbanized groups also assumes new forms—for example, the pluralistic interaction of different groups occupying the same area. A corollary to the proliferation of new social bases is the expansion of the number of groups of which any individual can be a member. Thus, the oblique interrelation of social groups in this type of urbanization precludes measurement in purely historicist terms. Such interrelations are not the simple result of successive phases as outlined, for example, in the Redfield-Singer model, in which primary urbanization, or adoption of sedentary residence that permits the formation of a single "great tradition," gives way to secondary urbanization, or contact with other cultures that eventually subsumes a multitude of "little traditions" (Redfield and Singer 1962:335–36). Instead, more empirically based terms are necessary for the recognition of an infinite number of juxtapositions beyond secondary urbanization and the dissolution of a hierarchical connection between great and little traditions.

More than many other processes of change, modernization and urbanization are especially relevant to a study of folk music during the past two centuries. Much of the technology that affects the transmission of folk music exists because of the industrial revolution. Even more important than specific objects of technology are the processes whereby all forms of technology are inexpensive and mass-produced. Almost anyone can easily procure a dulcimer or a banjo, a guitar or a fiddle. Our basic precepts for the combinations and hierarchies of social organization have also changed profoundly during the two hundred years since the French Revolution with its recasting of the modern, secular nation-state. We may take this relatively novel form of the nation-state for granted, but we do so only in conjunction with an acceptance of implicit and explicit concepts of national music. Welsh, German, or Kurdish folk musics are creations of the modern nationalistic imagination, and yet various groups stand ready to argue the reality and ancient roots of such musics. These transformations in the modern world have tended to skew the ways in which folk music canons form, yielding canons that no longer require any basis in ruralness or generation-to-generation transmission. The resulting conceptualizations of folk music in the modern world are certainly vaster, and indeed also richer.

Patterns of Change

The conservative nature of much folk music scholarship often projects the patterns of change resulting from modernization and urbanization in a negative light. When transported to the city, traditions die away; the mass media impoverish repertories and level style differences; true folk music exists only in an older, more innocent generation; modern society poses a very real threat of extinction. Closer examination of the persistence of folk music, however, does not justify this necrological stance. More commonly, patterns of change occur dialectically, with waning repertories being replaced by more vital ones and new, vibrant styles emerging when others lack the flexibility to withstand change. These dialectical patterns, therefore, account for change in a much more positive way, concentrating on the processes of ongoing change and accepting the ossification of some products as a natural result of that change.

An inevitable marker of musical change is a shift in the social basis of folk music. As the primacy of one form of social organization recedes, there is a realignment of previous groups and the formation of new groups with completely different social bases. The tremendous mobility characteristic of modern societies makes such realignments commonplace. Indeed, migration, even within rural areas, has long been a factor associated with musical change and the formation of new canons. Neil V. Rosenberg points out that the Piedmont region of the American South was subject to considerable shifting of population while remaining relatively as rural as other parts of the United States; nonetheless, the resulting musical and social confluence in the Piedmont made it a caldron for a degree of musical change that belies commonly held conceptions of the South as a bastion of musical stability and uniformity (Rosenberg 1985:20; cf. Denisoff 1973:15–23 and Wilgus 1971:137). The formation of new groups resulting from shifting populations has become one of the most fruitful areas of folk music study. In the United States, folk music study has increasingly concentrated on immigrant and ethnic studies. The meaningfulness of ethnicity as a central criterion for studying folk music style shows little sign of subsiding as large-scale immigration of Asians offers new perspectives for understanding the social basis of music in a pluralistic society (e.g., Jairazbhoy and DeVale 1985).

The changing social basis of folk music is seen not only in the emergence of new groups but also in the freedom with which individuals participate in more groups than one as the result of increasingly permeable social boundaries (Barth 1969:9–16). Accordingly, individuals encounter more than one musical repertory and type of musical behavior, both randomly and as a matter of choice (Royce 1982:185–88). Individuals toting quite different cultural baggage, "foreigners," cross social boundaries unchecked and are able to participate rather quickly in the cultural activities of the group, their distinctive contributions rarely discernible as a fillip to the status quo (Nettl 1985:163). It is exactly this foreign challenge to the status quo—so effectively obscured in the modern context—that wields tremendous potential for the formation of a new canon (Kenner 1984:369).

Shifting patterns of individual group membership mean that pluralism must be viewed both quantitatively and qualitatively. Pluralism becomes considerably more complicated than a mosaic with discrete parts—ethnic groups, for example—forming the whole. Instead, certain groups achieve influence outside their own boundaries. That is especially true of groups that gain greater control over the processes of urbanization. Serbo-Croatian folk music exerts a sort of hegemony in the musical life of Pittsburgh, where Serbo-Croatian musical organizations dominate in such diverse institutions as Duquesne University, home of the "Tamburitzans," and the Pittsburgh Folk Festival, whose organizers are almost exclusively Tamburitzan graduates (Haritan 1980). Folk music style, too, rides the coattails of modernization, with the result that some groups are willing to invest their interests in rather specific styles. Bluegrass is one of the best examples of a style that attracted a following from diverse groups by forging a tradition through the modern media of festivals, the urban folk music revival, records, and eventually television (Rosenberg 1983).

Another dialectical process of change has been the dissolution of the stratification of musical genres, with replacement by new patterns of generic interaction. Whether one accepts the historical legitimacy of stratification or not, it can be argued that social and historical distance did separate some aspects of folk and art music. With the growth of urbanization, however, that distance grew smaller and eventually disappeared. Thus, folk and art music do not occupy discrete strata. Even in the early nineteenth century, folk music in Central Europe was accorded artistic treatment, appearing in arrangements for large choruses and in collections intended for the scrutiny of scholarly investigators. Not surprisingly, the manipulation of folk music to approximate artistic ends assisted in a process of defining and inculcating nationalism. Ironically, nineteenth-century European concepts of nationalism depended on the ability of collectors and arrangers to demonstrate convincingly that the gap between folk and art music was not great. Folk music in these nationalistic exercises served as the link to a protonationalistic cultural unity, whereas its artistic reformulation was meant to traditionalize that unity in contemporary musical activity.

Modern folk music demonstrates a somewhat different interaction with popular music. This interaction has benefited from the proximity of the strata these two genres putatively occupied, both being the music of nonelite groups (Ivey 1982:133). Whatever technology's specific roles may be and whatever the extent of its mediation of popular music, many musicians have successfully controlled the popularization of folk music. Again, the history of bluegrass is illustrative of the ways in which the figurative fences between folk and popular music are carefully straddled. On one hand, bluegrass depends on the mass media to broaden its appeal and to create selective markets. On the other, bluegrass musicians judiciously defer to their "roots" in folk music in order to retain their "core audience," which now has a historical continuity quite independent of the various experiments in popularization to which bluegrass has been subject (Cantwell 1984:143–56).

One of the most subtle dialectical changes rendered by modernization produces a gradual transformation in the concepts of timelessness that attend folk music. In traditional society the age of a folk song has two markers, one definite and the other indefinite. Transmission provides the definite marker: the folk song's tenure in an individual musician's repertory begins when it is learned well enough to be performed. The indefinite marker derives from a general consensus that the song was known in an earlier generation, perhaps in association with a particular singer, and that it is probably much older than that. Replacing this concept of timelessness is one in which the past is consciously invoked to serve as a surrogate for the present. Tradition therefore comes into existence because of the fabrication of continuity with the past. The practice of constructing continuity by selectively choosing, and not infrequently selectively inventing, the past is a particularly modern phenomenon, dependent on its implicit collapse of time and space (Hobsbawm 1983:11–12). Folk songs thus become evocative symbols of the past, and they legitimize the traditionality of a contemporary context by virtue of their symbolic value. It is not important (or possible) that a specific historical moment and place be represented; nor is there any awareness that musical styles, genres, and repertories are juxtaposed in ways uncharacteristic of any past. Rather, folk music, because of its new timelessness, carries the weight of continuity and tradition.

Timelessness, however, does not negate the concern for authenticity; one might even say that the complete collapse of time is a necessary precursor to the invention of a new authenticity, with its specification of moment, event, and actor. The most glaring example of fabricating authenticity is the creation of Scottish Highland tradition in the imaginary personage of Ossian, who had presumably chronicled the early days of Highland tradition in epic and ballads actually composed by James Macpherson, a real eighteenth-century Scotsman (Trevor-Roper 1983); that Ossian should have given birth to a tradition filled with bagpipes and tartans is further evidence of the role timelessness plays in the establishment of tradition. Folk songs authenticating history continue to comprise one of the most common American genres of anthology, the premise of which is that folk song retains some deep-seated value that makes its historical tale constitute a "folksong heritage of America" (Knott 1953:143; cf. Darling 1983, Forcucci 1984, and Scott 1983).

Revival is an overt and explicit act of authentication. The revivalist not only identifies a specific time and place for folk music but is fundamentally concerned with recreating its value-laden social context. Folk music should suggest the nature of that social context while filling in some of the specific details to prove that authentication is part and parcel of revival. Real or not, these details have random and disconnected origins, and mustering them for the purposes of revival provides yet another guise for timelessness. Revival is, in an ideological sense, the ultimate collapse of time and space because it fully admits of the efficacy of that collapse for creating contemporary meaning. Revival relies heavily on new symbols masquerading as the old. Thus, when borrowing folk music from the past, the revivalist assumes that the audience will simultaneously imagine one set of values, strip those values from the music, and allow new, presumably immanent, values to assert themselves. The implied age and authenticity of revived folk music are often shifted to such external, nonmusical aspects as the naming of pieces or styles. The rubric "old-time," with its transparent assurance of age, is one of the most prevalent symbols of such a nonmusical aspect in American folk music. Those who perform country music, therefore, prefer to call it (or the roots it represents) "old-time" rather than "hillbilly"; more popularized subgenres of ethnic folk music similarly become ethnic "old-time" music, as if there were some fear that this was not the case.

Revival abates impoverishment by empowering even a reduced census of performers and organizers to identify specific musical activities as central to a tradition. Indeed, it is often because the census is small that revival, whatever its effectiveness, has particular urgency; Nettl has suggested that such is the case in the recent resurgence of traditional music in the Middle East (1985:157). Revival is inseparable from some of the most widespread contemporary institutions of folk music. Folk music festivals are essentially revivalistic; the donning of symbols that redirect cultural awareness to the past contributes to the spirit of revival. National music and nationalism overtly channel the revival of the past by suggesting a continuous connection to a historical stage of protonationhood. The practice of reissuing old recordings, especially early field recordings, puts technology at the service of revival. Even the institutionalization of written traditions of folk music results from the explicit goal of editors to spur revival, to make the folk music of the past live again in new forms of expression. Its effectiveness has made revival a prime means throughout the world of capturing the past in order to build traditions in the present (ibid.:162).

One final dialectical pattern of change characterizes the commodification of folk music. Commodification in this sense refers to the replacement of primary-group functions for folk music with circulation among many groups, whose ability to consume folk music does not depend on specific social function (Baumann 1976:65–67). In other words, folk music becomes a commodity with market value. Media develop for the production and sale of folk music, and remuneration comes from people with whom the folk musician has little or no contact. Only in theory does the musician have a sense of the specific cultural boundaries of his or her audience. Nonetheless, the folk musician endeavors to expand those boundaries, whether for ideological reasons—the message—or for reasons fundamental to the corporate structure of the recording industry.

Commodification inevitably leads to specialization and professionalization. Songwriters, arrangers, sound technicians, and festival organizers—all are professionals in the modernization of folk music. Quite simply, no single professional folk musician can manage all aspects of performance, so there results increasing dependence on specialization. Defining the folk community, then, is its ability to consume various specialties—to patronize coffeehouses or buy concert tickets, to concentrate interest on bluegrass or limit it to ethnic folk music. Its repertory and "original" functions notwithstanding, folk music often becomes popular music. Its relation to a public—a folk community—is not ostensibly different from that of popular music, even if the audiences are often smaller. Perhaps galling to advocates of a more pristine cultural role for folk music, commodification has, nevertheless, secured new audiences and new social contexts for folk music in the modern world.

Responses to Change

If folk music undergoes general patterns of change because of modernization, the responses of specific musicians and communities are often quite contrasting. Revival might best be achieved by several responses, depending on the goals of a particular community and the means of response it has at its disposal. More often than not, these responses overlap, again according to the specific community they come to characterize. Even in the vague dialectics that the following order suggests with pairs like consolidation and diversification, popularization and classicization, I mean to suggest that seemingly opposing responses may well complement each other. The rather positive tenor that follows in the discussion of these various responses is intended as exactly that. I do not intend this tenor to conceal changes that others would construe as negative: impoverishment, abandonment, extinction of repertory. But my concern here is with responses—conscious actions on the part of musician and community to stave off, redirect, or intensify change—rather than with the forces that bring about these responses. Thus, it is arguable that a consolidated repertory exemplifies impoverishment, but when a community concentrates its repertory in order to preserve certain value-laden pieces, this becomes a response that arrests impoverishment. Some might regard popularization as an abandonment of traditional social contexts; but as a response popularization expands the existing social contexts and creates more inclusive, rather than exclusive, audiences for folk music.

Consolidation results from the identification of salient aspects within the tradition—whether repertory, style, or social venue—and the consequent concentration on these aspects. An anthology of folk songs consolidates by claiming they are *deutsche Volkslieder* or "the English and Scottish popular ballads." Delimiting the instrumentarium also consolidates, thereby allowing musicians to concentrate on refined technique or virtuosity, as is the case with the mandolin in bluegrass. Social transformations also lend themselves to consolidation. German-American immigrants in the nineteenth century concentrated their repertories of folk songs in several publication formats, all of which stripped away differences in dialect and variation, and they superseded these repertories with a core of songs in *Hochdeutsch*. The egalitarian, restrictive slot on a folk-festival stage ("twenty minutes for each act") forces consolidation, albeit a form accompanied by a sense that this slot encapsulates the essence of Polish-American folk song or West Virginia clog-dancing. At the musical level, consolidation often takes the form of synthesis or syncretism, which permits the emergence of an innovative style, leading to an overall expansion of the repertory—in other words, to diversification (Waterman 1952 and Nettl 1978:133).

Diversification is in many ways the obverse of consolidation, for it is less concerned with the salience of tradition than with the quantity and breadth of the performance. Modern folk music ensembles therefore perform in many, often unrelated styles. Other ensembles purposely seek to diversify their instrumentarium. Consolidation and diversification may accompany each other. Contemporary German folk musicians, for example, exhibit a tendency to make one of two choices regarding dialect repertories (Paulin 1980:24). On one hand, some musicians consolidate by concentrating on a single regional dialect (for example, Michael Bauer on *pfälzisch*); on the other, there are musicians who sing in several dialects (for example, *Zupfgeigenhansl*). Modernized concepts of musical tradition both tolerate and encourage diversification. Country music regularly combines traditional, religious, and popular elements, tempering them even more with styles drawn from bluegrass or ethnic "old-time" music. Diversification consciously spawns musical pluralism.

The biographies of contemporary musicians often bear witness to a path that begins with a traditional orientation to folk music but moves ineluctably in the direction of popularization. This general path would threaten the generic correlation between folk and popular music, if in fact many professionals did not choose to pause and maintain that correlation. Thus, bluegrass remains overall a mixture of folk and popular music, despite the very real opportunities to capitulate to the pressures and seduction of popular culture (cf. Cantwell

1984:1–18). Popularization in a different sense is very important in the revival and invention of folk music tradition, which require popular acceptance of sweeping representations of musical styles for which little or no firsthand familiarity is available.

Classicization and Westernization are two responses that differ somewhat from popularization because of the genres they normally combine. In general, folk musicians do not demonstrate a tendency toward becoming art musicians or performing art music, although more do in Western than in non-Western contexts. Modernization, nevertheless, has long encouraged the influences of Western art music. Harmonization and arrangement for chorus was a normal component of the public dissemination of folk music in nineteenth-century Germany; these techniques legitimized folk music by stressing its general compatibility with traditions of art music (Baumann 1976:66–67). The display of virtuosity by many folk musicians is also evidence of the desire to perform as one would in Western art music (Nettl 1985:137–38). Classicization also betokens a connection with the past, and in so doing it becomes a frequent handmaiden of nationalism, despite its external universality.

Institutionalization includes a number of responses, all of which result in the reformulation of groups to maintain folk music tradition. Institutionalization may effect the appearance of new ensembles or the emergence of new functions for older groups. In many German-American communities in the Midwest, church choirs regularly performed in social contexts outside the church, combining their staple religious repertory with secular folk songs. Institutional undergirding extended thereby to both sacred and secular repertories of German-American music (Bohlman 1984b). Growing literacy often produces various forms of institutionalization. Literacy, in effect, creates a number of cultural types who participate in the institutionalization of folk music: collectors, editors, publishers, teachers, chorus directors, even accompanists. The study of folk music also institutionalizes by providing places and methodologies that enable scholars to examine folk music in systematic ways.

Specialization affects virtually all aspects of folk music in the modern world. In certain ways, this response is the binary opposite of institutionalization, for it reflects a proliferation of individuals involved in the maintenance of tradition. Specialization results when an individual acquires and exercises special skills that fit in with a larger whole. Institutionalization also encourages the acquisition of special skills but tends to organize them hierarchically in relation to organizations. Clearly necessary for the professional basis of some folk music activities, specialization is also a component of the choices necessary for juxtaposing repertories and articulating the need to revive and authenticate.

With folk music extirpated from primary functions in small groups and communities, new cohesive functions form, and many of these functions, especially when they are the products of specialists, result from ideologization. Even though new cohesive functions may theoretically assume myriad forms, they tend to exist empirically in rather specific ways, reflecting the cultural, political, and musical concerns of a specialized group. The breakdown of the rural, agrarian populace has stimulated many English folk song scholars to resituate the social basis of folk music in the urban, industrialized working class (Lloyd 1967:316–411 and Harker 1985:231–32; cf. Keil 1982:58 and Greenway 1953:5–10). Ideologically, this argument replaces one form of stratification with another, which is tempered by British Marxian historiography. The encouragement of ethnic folk music in many American communities often rests on the notion that certain conservative social institutions should centralize the musical culture of the ethnic community. Comprising the core of many Eastern European ethnic communities in Pittsburgh, for example, is the Catholic church, albeit its ethnic American version. In this version Pittsburgh Slovaks revive both Slovak folk dance and the mass in Slovak by coupling the performance of folk dance troupes with religion at special city-wide gatherings; presiding over Slovak folk festival days is always a priest, who continually draws attention to the ideological basis of Slovak folk music in America: the church and its teachings, with their special meaning for Slovak-Americans. Nationalism is one of the most extreme and pervasive manifestations of ideologization. The specific ideological symbols of nationalistic folk music—for example, those chosen to represent the German *Wandervogel* youth movement (the camaraderie of youth, wandering in nature, and the guitar as the musical instrument of the German *Volk*)—may be relatively few, but they are nevertheless conceived to specify the ideology of nationhood as directly as possible. Ideology determines the ways in which time and place collapse and how the musical activities that result from this collapse articulate a specific message to a specific group. Ideologization serves, therefore, as a response that invests even more meaning and symbolism in folk music than it might otherwise convey.

Folk Music in the Modern World: Some Fundamental Corollaries

The performance of the "Zum Lauterbach hab' ich mein' Strumpf verlor'n" medley (example 10) demonstrates many of the salient qualities of folk music in the modern world. Both text and context reveal the permeation of modernization throughout the tradition of which the song is a part. Interpretation of some aspects of the performance, such as the persistence of German-language songs in the United States, would suggest that the tradition is conservative; other aspects—the adaptation of the "blues-yodeling" style of Jimmie Rodgers, for example—challenge that interpretation of conservatism, making us wonder whether we are really observing the deterioration of ethnic tradition and the unmitigated encroachment of popular music. Neither interpretation is really wrong; neither is really correct. "Zum Lauterbach" juxtaposes a remarkable range of elements from a complex traditional framework, rendering modernism a normative context for the performer, his audience, and the community of which they are a part.

The area of eastern Wisconsin in which "Zum Lauterbach" was recorded in 1984 has contained a large German population since the mid-nineteenth century. German folk music traditions have long flourished in the area, and "Zum Lauterbach" must qualify as one of the best-known German songs. Its transmission takes place in numerous subgenres, ranging from fairly straightforward vocal versions to complex arrangements for the hundreds of "Dutchman" bands that play throughout the Upper Midwest. In short, it is hardly surprising to discover singers in this German-American region who know "Zum Lauterbach." Why, then, the Jimmie Rodgers style? Why the truncated version? How can we account for the other songs that are appended, one of them in English and rather banal?

Close analysis of "Zum Lauterbach" reveals that this performance makes sense, that is, the seemingly disparate and unrelated parts fit together to yield a logical whole. The logic of this whole, however, depends on a broadly accepted concept of modernization in the canon. We have already established that the German text and melody of "Zum Lauterbach" is well known in the region. So, too, is the singing style and the larger genre and repertory with which it is inextricably associated: country-western music. The singer, much enamored of Jimmie Rodgers, adapts the Singing Brakeman's style with relative success. The guitar accompaniment simplifies the style in order to make it unobtrusive, so it will not conflict with the German songs; it is the yodeling that confirms the style, and it does so by clearly framing other musical elements. The synthesis of melodic, rhythmic, and harmonic elements clearly demonstrates syncretism. The melodies are similar in structure, phrasing, and overall contour; melodically, one almost has the sense of variant verses of the same song. The rhythm is flexible enough to allow alteration, and the harmonic similarity of different sections reinforces the feeling of a repeated structural pattern. The yodeling, though it might conflict with the unity of the performance, actually enhances

Zum Lauterbach hab' ich mein' Strumpf verlor'n

Singer: Albert Kolberg   Sheboygan County, Wisconsin
Source: Martin et al. 1986: side 1, cut 1   13 December 1984
                                        Collected by Philip Martin
                                    Transcribed by Christine W. Bohlman

EXAMPLE 10

Translation

"Zum Lauterbach"

In Lauterbach I lost my stockings,
And without stockings I'm not going home.
So I'm going back to Lauterbach,
To get some stockings for my legs.

"Mein Hut"

My hat, it has three corners.
Three corners has my hat.
And if a hat does not have three corners,
Then it is not my hat.

EXAMPLE 10 (Cont.)

that unity by outlining the harmonic structures that accompany each of the texted sections.

The sources of the song's components seem at first to be incompatible, but here, too, the logic of the whole eliminates the differences of the parts. "Mein Hut, der hat drei Ecken" is as familiar to the German-Americans of the region as "Zum Lauterbach." It also has incarnations in a wide range of traditional subgenres. If we regard the blues yodeling as intrinsic to the style, "Where, Oh Where, Did My Little Dog Go?" has perhaps the most anomalous source of the various components in this performance. It probably did not come directly from Jimmie Rodgers. We cannot be sure that Rodgers never performed the song, but a recorded version of it is unknown (Porterfield 1979:378–429); we can safely say, then, that the singer is not mimicking Jimmie Rodgers, as he was wont to do otherwise. "Where, Oh Where" is simply lifted from a more general popular music repertory that circulated in eastern Wisconsin, a repertory with only tangential connections to country-western.

The context that makes this pastiche of style and repertory possible is the radio. The singer performs frequently on local radio, a medium that permits him remarkable stylistic peregrination. Some audiences will pick and choose which styles and repertories they prefer, but overall the region's pluralism results in musical tolerance. It broadcasts a tradition with very diverse facets. The ethnic and socioeconomic complexity of eastern Wisconsin, therefore, makes a folk song like "Zum Lauterbach" possible. Historical moment, place, style, ethnicity, and genre—all conjoin around the song, and in so doing they reshape its many parts into a whole that is perfectly recognizable and meaningful to the folk musician and his community.

To accept the existence of folk music in the modern world requires a reformulation of many of the conservative theories that scholars and ideologues have long used to delimit folk music as a genre. It requires that we amend intractable notions of isolation, ruralness, purely oral tradition, and primary function; those unwilling to do so have few choices but to track down vestiges or to reshuffle the pages of older collections. These would seem to be particularly thankless tasks, given the diversity that modernization has stimulated.

The relation of folk music to its social basis in the modern world has grown more complex. Regardless of size, single groups have come to regard more than one kind of music as their own. A corollary of this expansion of social basis is that a single repertory of folk music is no longer the property of a single group or community. Even when a community shares relatively the same styles and repertories, these contain aspects that come from different sources. Moreover, the social basis of folk music is continuously in flux, with groups altering their concepts of the ways in which musical style and social behavior shape their folk music canons. Musical activity, in some cases, has come to define the subgroup, rather than the subgroup defining its musical practices. Thus, ensembles may come into existence to perform ethnic music at folk festivals or public ethnic events, even when there are no clear contexts elsewhere. New contexts may emerge as festival ensembles diversify to provide the necessary catalyst for a transformation from subgroup to folk music community, with the latter developing a broad foundation for the support of its own musical culture.

Stratification is no longer a meaningful designation of folk music as a genre. Separation of musical genres into strata of folk, popular, religious, and art or, alternatively, into class structures results from aesthetic and political exclusiveness and avoids the empirical consideration of musical change. It is still possible to separate elements of folk and popular music, but we most often encounter them in a state of confluence. The distinguishing marks of art music—innovation, complex combinations of simultaneous sounds, virtuosity—also influence many folk musicians. Finally, the increasing presence of non-Western music, in which stratification may be irrelevant as a generic label for folk music, undermines the past tendency to reduce folk music to an idealized stratum devoid of change.

The performance of folk music is rarely not specialized. Performers develop special skills and concentrate on specialized repertories. The different responses to change result in many patterns of specialization, patterns that may cross the threshold into professionalization, consolidate a personalized style, or draw attention to a specific ideological position. Like the performer, the audience is specialized, sometimes along more traditional lines, as in the intensification of interest in one's own ethnic music, and sometimes along the lines of patronage of institutions that specialize in the cultivation of specific subgenres.

Both oral and written tradition become more complex. Modernization is not, in fact, the supplanting of oral tradition by written tradition. The greater diversity of folk music requires that the aural responses to folk music be both broader and more refined. The community and the audience engage in oral processes of interpreting their canons. Written traditions, too, are not reducible to the use of musical notation. Folk musicians use written traditions in various ways, some as merely a rough outline, others as a means of rapid learning, still others to expedite ensemble performance. Technology often combines oral and written traditions. A recorded performance, therefore, provides a fixed type of written text, yet one that musicians learn from orally.

The many contexts of folk music in the modern world mean that musical change occurs multidimensionally. Musical change ceases to observe deterministic paths of development, along which specific causes yield predictable effects. Linear interpretation of musical change would never predict the version of "Zum Lauterbach" that actually emerged. Such a performance results from influences that are both random and carefully invested with meaning for a specific group. This confluence of randomness and specific agenda has forged a new folk song—one can justifiably say a unique song whose cultural locus is in a multidimensional tradition that modernization has made possible by collapsing time and space. The elements of "Zum Lauterbach" are related, but not because of a shared cultural message and not because of similar temporal origins. Instead, their relatedness depends on a heterogeneous assortment of hybrid styles and juxtaposed cultural values, all of them tempered by the community's extensive tolerance of the expressive potential of folk music in the modern world.

BIBLIOGRAPHY

Abrahams, Roger D., ed. 1970. *A Singer and Her Songs*. Baton Rouge: Louisiana State University Press.
———.1972. "Personal Power and Social Restraint in the Definition of Folklore." In Américo Paredes and Richard Bauman, eds., *Toward New Perspectives in Folklore*. Austin: University of Texas Press.
Abrahams, Roger D., and George Foss. 1968. *Anglo-American Folksong Style*. Englewood Cliffs, N.J.: Prentice-Hall.
al Faruqi, Lois Ibsen. 1981a. *An Annotated Glossary of Arabic Musical Terms*. Westport, Conn.: Greenwood Press.
———.1981b. "The Status of Music in Muslim Nations: Evidence from the Arab World." *Asian Music* 12 (1):56–85.
———.1985. "Music, Musicians and Muslim Law." *Asian Music* 17(1):3–36.
Altieri, Charles. 1984. "An Idea and Ideal of a Literary Canon." In Robert von Hallberg, ed., *Canons*. Chicago: University of Chicago Press.
Anderson, Benedict. 1983. *Imagined Communities: Reflections on the Origin and Spread of Nationalism*. London: Verso.
Arnim, Achim von, and Clemens Brentano. 1980. *Des Knaben Wunderhorn: Alte deutsche Lieder*. Munich: Winkler. Originally published 1806–8.
Attali, Jacques. 1985. *Noise: The Political Economy of Music*. Trans. by Brian Massumi. Minneapolis: University of Minnesota Press.
Austin, J.L. 1975. *How To Do Things with Words*. Ed. by J.O. Urmson and Marina Sbisà. Cambridge, Mass.: Harvard University Press.
Barkechli, Mehdi. 1963. *La musique traditionelle de l'Iran*. Teheran: Secretariat d'état aux beaux-arts.
Barry, Phillips. 1914. "The Transmission of Folk-Song," *Journal of American Folklore* 27:67–76.
———.1933. "Communal Re-Creation." *Bulletin of the Folk-Song Society of the Northeast* 5:4–6.
———.1961. "The Part of the Folk Singer in the Making of Folk Balladry." In MacEdward Leach and Tristram P. Coffin, eds., *The Critics and the Ballad*. Carbondale: Southern Illinois University Press.
———1987. "Some Aspects of Folk-Song." *Journal of American Folklore* 100: 70–79. Originally published in *Journal of American Folklore* 25 (1912):274–83.
Barth, Fredrik, ed. 1969. *Ethnic Groups and Boundaries: The Social Organization of Ethnic Groups*. Boston: Little, Brown.
Bartók, Béla. 1920. "Die Volksmusik der Araber von Biskra und Umgebung," *Zeitschrift für Musikwissenschaft* 2:489–522.
———.1931. *Hungarian Folk Music*. Trans. by M.C. Calvacoressi. London: Oxford University Press.
———.1972a. "Ungarische Volksmusik und neue ungarische Musik," In Bence Szabolcsi, ed., *Béla Bartók: Weg und Werk*. Munich: Deutscher Taschenbuch Verlag.
———.1972b. "Vom Einfluß der Bauernmusik auf die Musik unserer Zeit." In Bence Szabolcsi, ed., *Béla Bartók: Weg und Werk*. Munich: Deutscher Taschenbuch Verlag.

————.1976. *Turkish Folk Music from Asia Minor.* Princeton, N.J.: Princeton University Press.

Basso, Ellen B. 1985. A *Musical View of the Universe: Kalapalo Myth and Ritual Performances.* Philadelphia: University of Pennsylvania Press.

Bauman, Richard. 1972. "Differential Identity and the Social Basis of Folklore." In Américo Paredes and Richard Bauman, eds., *Toward New Perspectives in Folklore.* Austin: University of Texas Press.

Baumann, Max Peter. 1976. *Musikfolklore und Musikfolklorismus: Eine ethnomusikologische Untersuchung zum Funktionswandel des Jodels.* Winterthur: Amadeus.

Bausinger, Hermann. 1980. *Formen der "Volkspoesie."* 2d rev. ed. Berlin: Erich Schmidt.

Bayard, Samuel P. 1950. "Prolegomena to a Study of the Principal Melodic Families of British-American Folk Song." *Journal of American Folklore* 63:1–44.

————.1953. "American Folksongs and Their Music." *Southern Folklore Quarterly* 17:130–38.

————.1954. "Two Representative Tune Families of British Tradition." *Midwest Folklore* 4:13–34.

Belden, H.M., ed. 1973. *Ballads and Songs Collected by the Missouri Folk-Lore Society.* Columbia: University of Missouri Press.

Benjamin, Walter. 1969. "The Work of Art in the Age of Mechanical Reproduction." In idem, *Illuminations: Essays and Reflections.* Ed. by Hannah Arendt. Trans. by Harry Zorn. New York: Schocken.

Bielawski, Ludwik. 1973(?). "Formale Aspekte der Ordnungsmethoden bei Volksliedweisen." In Doris Stockmann and Jan Stęszewski, eds., *Analyse und Klassifikation von Volksmelodien.* Kraków: Polskie Wydawnictwo Muzyczne.

Blacking, John. 1957. *The Role of Music amongst the Venda of the Northern Transvaal.* Johannesburg: International Library of African Music.

————.1973. *How Musical Is Man?* Seattle: University of Washington Press.

————.1981. "Making Artistic Popular Music: The Goal of True Folk." *Popular Music* 1:9–14.

Blum, Stephen. 1972. "The Concept of the ᶜAsheq in Northern Khorasan." *Asian Music* 4 (1):27–47.

————.1974. "Persian Folksong in Meshhed (Iran), 1969." *Yearbook of the International Folk Music Council* 6:86–114.

Boehm, Johanen. 1971. "Music in Modern Israel" ["Music"]. *Encyclopaedia Judaica.* Vol. 12, columns 669–70. Jerusalem: Keter.

Bohlman, Philip V. 1980. "The Folk Songs of Charles Bannen: The Interaction of Music and History in Southwestern Wisconsin." *Transactions of the Wisconsin Academy of Sciences, Arts and Letters* 68:167–87.

————.1982. " 'Viele Einwanderer aus der alten Welt': German-American Rural Community Structure in Wisconsin." *Midwestern Journal of Language and Folklore* 8 (1):8–33.

————.1984a. "The Musical Culture of Central European Jewish Immigrants to Israel." Ph.D. dissertation, University of Illinois at Urbana-Champaign.

————.1984b. "Hymnody in the Rural German-American Community of the Upper Midwest." *The Hymn* 35 (3):158–64.

————.1985. "Prolegomena to the Classification of German-American Music." *Yearbook of German-American Studies* 20:33–48.

Borges, Jorge Luis. 1964. "A New Refutation of Time." In idem, *Labyrinths: Selected Stories and Other Writings.* Ed. by Donald A. Yates and James E. Irby. New York: New Directions.

Brăiloiu, Constantin. 1984. *Problems of Ethnomusicology.* Ed. and trans. by A.L. Lloyd. Cambridge: Cambridge University Press.

Braun, Hartmut. 1982–83. "Beethoven und das Volkslied." *Jahrbuch für Volksliedforschung* 27–28:285–91.

Brednich, Rolf Wilhelm, and Wolfgang Suppan, eds. 1969. *Gottscheer Volkslieder.* 2 vols. Mainz: B. Schotts Söhne.

Brednich, Rolf Wilhelm, Lutz Röhrich, and Wolfgang Suppan, eds. 1973 and 1975. *Handbuch des Volksliedes.* 2 vols. Munich: Wilhelm Fink Verlag.

Brod, Max. 1976. *Die Musik Israels.* Rev. and expanded by Yehuda Walter Cohen. Kassel: Bärenreiter.

Bronson, Bertrand Harris. 1959–72. *The Traditional Tunes of the Child Ballads.* 4 vols. Princeton, N.J.: Princeton University Press.

————.1969. "Folk-Song and the Modes." In idem, ed., *The Ballad as Song.* Berkeley: University of California Press.

————.1972. "Are the Modes Outmoded?" *Yearbook of the International Folk Music Council* 4:23–31.

Brunvand, Jan Harold. 1986. *The Study of American Folklore: An Introduction.* 3d ed. New York: Norton.

Cantwell, Robert. 1984. *Bluegrass Breakdown: The Making of the Old Southern Sound.* Urbana: University of Illinois Press.

Capwell, Charles. 1986. *The Music of the Bauls of Bengal.* Kent, Ohio: Kent State University Press.

Cazden, Norman. 1971. "A Simplified Mode Classification for Traditional Anglo-American Song Tunes." *Yearbook of the International Folk Music Council* 3:45–78.

Child, Frances James. 1882–98. *The English and Scottish Popular Ballads.* 5 vols. Boston: Houghton, Mifflin.

Coffin, Tristram P. 1961. " 'Mary Hamilton' and the Anglo-American Ballad as an Art Form." In MacEdward Leach and Tristram P. Coffin, eds., *The Critics and the Ballad.* Carbondale: Southern Illinois University Press.

Cohen, Erik, and Amnon Shiloah. 1985. "Major Trends of Change in Jewish Oriental Ethnic Music in Israel," *Popular Music* 5:199–223.

Committee for Palestinian Folklore and Social Research. 1986. *The Middle East and South Asia Folklore Newsletter* 3 (2):2–4.

Culler, Jonathan. 1984. *On Deconstruction: Theory and Criticism after Structuralism.* Ithaca, N.Y.: Cornell University Press.

Curtis, Natalie. 1907. *The Indians' Book: An Offering by the American Indians of Indian Lore, Musical and Narrative, to Form a Record of the Songs and Legends of Their Race.* New York: Harper and Brothers.

Danckert, Werner. 1966. *Das Volkslied im Abendland.* Bern: Francke.

————.1970. *Das europäische Volkslied.* Bonn: H. Bouvier. First published 1937.

Danielson, Larry. 1977. Introduction. *Studies in Folklore and Ethnicity.* Special edition of *Western Folklore* 36 (1):1–5.

Darling, Charles W. 1983. *The New American Songster: Traditional Ballads and Songs of North America.* Lanham, Md.: University Press of America.

Denisoff, R. Serge. 1973. *Great Day Coming: Folk Music and the American Left.* Baltimore: Penguin.

Dessauer, Renata. 1928. *Das Zersingen: Ein Beitrag zur Psychologie des deutschen Volksliedes. (Germanische Studien* 61). Berlin: E. Ebering.

The Diagram Group. 1978. *Musical Instruments of the World.* New York: Bantam.

Dundes, Alan. 1965. *The Study of Folklore.* Englewood Cliffs, N.J.: Prentice-Hall.

————.1984. "Defining Identity through Folklore." *Journal of Folklore Research* 21 (2–3):149–52.

Dyen, Doris J., and Philip V. Bohlman. 1985. "Becoming Ethnic in Western Pennsylvania: Processes of Ethnic Identification in Pittsburgh and Its Environs." Paper delivered at the Annual Meeting of the American Folklore Society, Cincinnati.

Eckstorm, F.H. and Phillips Barry. 1930. "What Is Tradition?" *Bulletin of the Folk-Song Society of the Northeast* 1:2–3.

Editorial. 1949. *Journal of the International Folk Music Council* 1:1–2.

Elbourne, R.P. 1975. "The Question of Definition," *Yearbook of the International Folk Music Council* 7:9–29.

Erdely, Stephen. 1965. *Methods and Principles of Hungarian Ethnomusicology.* Bloomington: Indiana University Press.

Erk, Ludwig, ed. 1893–94. *Deutscher Liederhort.* 3 vols. Ed. and expanded by Franz Magnus Böhme. Leipzig: Breitkopf und Härtel.

Farmer, Henry George. 1967. *A History of Arabian Music to the XIIIth Century.* London: Luzac. First published 1929.

Feld, Steven. 1982. *Sound and Sentiment: Birds, Weeping, Poetics, and Song in Kaluli Expression.* Philadelphia: University of Pennsylvania Press.

Forcucci, Samuel L. 1984. *A Folk Song History of America: America through Its Songs.* Englewood Cliffs, N.J.: Prentice-Hall.

Forkel, Johann Nicolaus. 1788. *Allgemeine Geschichte der Musik.* Vol. 1. Leipzig: Schwickert.

Forry, Mark E. 1986. "The 'Festivalization' of Tradition in Yugoslavia." Paper read at the 31st Annual Meeting of the Society for Ethnomusicology, Rochester, N.Y.

Frey, J. William. 1960. "The Amish Hymns as Folk Music." In George Korson, ed., *Pennsylvania Songs and Legends.* Baltimore: Johns Hopkins University Press.

Geertz, Clifford. 1973. *The Interpretation of Cultures: Selected Essays.* New York: Basic Books.

———.1983. "Blurred Genres: The Refiguration of Social Thought." In idem, *Local Knowledge: Further Essays in Interpretive Anthropology.* New York: Basic Books.

General Report. 1953. *Journal of the International Folk Music Council* 5:9–35.

Glassie, Henry. 1970. " 'Take That Night Train to Selma': An Excursion to the Outskirts of Scholarship." In idem, Edward D. Ives, and John F. Szwed, eds., *Folksongs and Their Makers.* Bowling Green, Ohio: Bowling Green University Popular Press.

Goffman, Erving. 1967. *Interaction Ritual: Essays on Face-to-Face Behavior.* Garden City, N.Y.: Anchor Books.

Goja, Hermann. 1920. "Das Zersingen der Volkslieder: Ein Beitrag zur Psychologie der Volksdichtung." *Imago* 6:132–242.

Goldstein, Kenneth S. 1982. "The Impact of Recording Technology on the British Folksong Revival," In William Ferris and Mary L. Hart, eds., *Folk Music and Modern Sound.* Jackson: University Press of Mississippi.

Grabar, Oleg. 1973. *The Formation of Islamic Art.* New Haven, Conn: Yale University Press.

Greenway, John. 1953. *American Folksongs of Protest.* Philadelphia: University of Pennsylvania Press.

Gronow, Pekka. 1982. "Ethnic Recordings: An Introduction," In *Ethnic Recordings in America: A Neglected Heritage.* Washington, D.C.: Library of Congress.

Gummere, Francis B. 1907. *The Popular Ballad.* Boston and New York: Houghton, Mifflin.

———.1961. "The Ballad and Communal Poetry." In MacEdward Leach and Tristram P. Coffin, eds., *The Critics and the Ballad.* Carbondale: Southern Illinois University Press.

Gundlach, Willi. 1969. *Die Schulliederbücher von Ludwig Erk.* Cologne: Arno Volk.

von Hallberg, Robert. 1984. "Introduction." In Robert von Hallberg, ed., *Canons.* Chicago: University of Chicago Press.

Hanna, Judith Lynne. 1979. *To Dance Is Human: A Theory of Nonverbal Communication.* Austin: University of Texas Press.

Harich-Schneider, Eta. 1959. "The Last Remnants of a Mendicant Musicians' Guild: The *Goze* in Northern Honshu (Japan)." *Journal of the International Folk Music Council* 11:56–59.

Haritan, Michael Elarion. 1980. "History of the Pittsburgh Folk Festival, 1956–1979." Master's thesis, Duquesne University.

Harker, Dave. 1985. *Fakesong: The Manufacture of British "Folksong" 1700 to the Present Day.* Milton Keynes, England: Open University Press.

Hattox, Ralph S. 1985. *Coffee and Coffeehouses: The Origins of a Social Beverage in the Medieval Near East.* Seattle: University of Washington Press.

Hebdige, Dick. 1979. *Subculture: The Meaning of Style.* London: Methuen.

Herder, Johann Gottfried. 1975. *"Stimmen der Völker in Liedern": Volkslieder.* 2 vols. Stuttgart: Reclam. First published 1778–79.

Herzog, George. 1935. "Plains Ghost Dance and Great Basin Music." *American Anthropologist* 37:403–19.

———.1937. "Musical Typology in Folksong." *Southern Folklore Quarterly* 1 (2):49–55.

———.1949–50. "Song: Folk Song and the Music of Folk Song." In Maria Leach, ed., *Funk and Wagnalls Standard Dictionary of Folklore, Mythology, and Legend.* New York: Funk and Wagnalls.

Hitti, Philip K. 1970. *Islam: A Way of Life.* Chicago: Regnery Gateway.

Hobsbawm, Eric. 1983. "Introduction: Inventing Traditions." In idem and Terence Ranger, eds., *The Invention of Tradition.* Cambridge: Cambridge University Press.

Hood, Mantle. 1959. "The Reliability of Oral Tradition." *Journal of the American Musicological Society* 12 (2–3):201–9.

Hornbostel, Erich M. von, and Curt Sachs. 1961. "Classification of Musical Instruments." Trans. by Anthony Baines and Klaus P. Wachsmann. *Galpin Society Journal* 14:3–29.

Hostetler, John A. 1980. *Amish Society.* 3d ed. Baltimore: Johns Hopkins University Press.

Hymes, Dell. 1975. "Folklore's Nature and the Sun's Myth." *Journal of American Folklore* 88:345–69.

Idelsohn, A. Z. 1914–32. *Hebräisch-orientalischer Melodienschatz.* 10 vols. Leipzig: Benjamin Harz.

———.1967. *Jewish Music in Its Historical Development.* New York: Schocken.

The International Folk Music Council: Its Formation and Progress. 1949. *Journal of the International Folk Music Council* 1:3–4.

Ives, Edward D. 1964. *Larry Gorman: The Man Who Made the Songs.* Bloomington: Indiana University Press.

———.1978 *Joe Scott: The Woodsman-Songmaker.* Urbana: University of Illinois Press.

———.1983. "The Study of Regional Songs and Ballads." In Richard M. Dorson, ed., *Handbook of American Folklore.* Bloomington: Indiana University Press.

Ivey, William. 1952. "Commercialization and Tradition in the Nashville Sound." In William Ferris and Mary L. Hunt, eds., *Folk Music and Modern Sound.* Jackson: University Press of Mississippi.

Jairazbhoy, Nazir A., and Sue Carole DeVale, eds. 1985. *Asian Music in North America. Selected Reports in Ethnomusicology* 6.

Kadman, Gurit. 1968. *The New Israeli Folkdances.* [Tel Aviv]: [Histadrut].

Karpeles, Maud. 1951. "Reflections on Authenticity in Folk Music." *Journal of the International Folk Music Council* 3:10–16.

Kartomi, Margaret J. 1981. "The Processes and Results of Musical Culture Contact: A Discussion of Terminology and Concepts." *Ethnomusicology* 25 (2):227–49.

Kealiinohomoku, Joann Wheeler. 1972. "Folk Dance." In Richard M. Dorson, ed., *Folklore and Folklife: An Introduction.* Chicago: University of Chicago Press.

Keil, Charles. 1966. *Urban Blues.* Chicago: University of Chicago Press.

———.1978. "Who Needs 'the Folk'?" *Journal of the Folklore Institute* 15 (3):263–65.

———.1982. "Slovenian Style in Milwaukee." In William Ferris and Mary L. Hart, eds., *Folk Music and Modern Sound.* Jackson: University Press of Mississippi.

Kenner, Hugh. 1984. "The Making of the Modernist Canon." In Robert von Hallberg, ed., *Canons.* Chicago: University of Chicago Press.

Keren, Zvi. 1980. *Contemporary Israeli Music: Its Sources and Stylistic Developments.* Ramat-Gan, Israel: Bar Ilan University Press.

Kermode, Frank. 1985. *Forms of Attention.* Chicago: University of Chicago Press.

Kirshenblatt-Gimblett, Barbara. 1983. "Studying Immigrant and Ethnic Folklore." In Richard M. Dorson, ed., *Handbook of American Folklore.* Bloomington: Indiana University Press.

Kivy, Peter. 1984. *Sound and Semblance: Reflections on Musical Representation.* Princeton, N.J.: Princeton University Press.

Kleeman, Janice E. 1985–86. "The Parameters of Musical Transmission." *The Journal of Musicology* 4 (2):1–22.

Klusen, Ernst. 1969. *Volkslied: Fund und Erfindung.* Cologne: Gerig.

———1973. "Das sozialkritische Lied." In Rolf Wilhelm Brednich, Lutz Röhrich, and Wolfgang Suppan, eds., *Handbuch des Volksliedes.* Vol. 1: *Die Gattungen des Volksliedes.* Munich: Wilhelm Fink.

———1986. "The Group Song as Object." In James R. Dow and Hannjost Lixfeld, eds. and translators, *German Volkskunde: A Decade of Theoretical Confrontation, Debate, and Reorientation (1967–1977).* Bloomington: Indiana University Press.

Klymasz, Robert B. 1972. " 'Sounds You Never Heard Before': Ukrainian Country Music in Western Canada." *Ethnomusicology* 16 (5):372–80.

Knott, Sarah Gertrude. 1953. "The Folk Festival Movement in America." *Southern Folklore Quarterly* 17 (2):143–55.

Kodály, Zoltán. 1960. *Folk Music of Hungary.* Trans. by Ronald Tempest and Cynthia Jolly. London: Barrie and Rockliff.

Kolinski, Mieczyslaw. 1968. " 'Barbara Allen': Tonal Versus Melodic Structure, Part I." *Ethnomusicology* 12 (2):208–18.

———.1969. " 'Barbara Allen': Tonal versus Melodic Structure, Part II." *Ethnomusicology* 13 (1):1–73.

Koller, Oswald. 1902–3. "Die beste Methode, volks- und volksmässige Lieder nach ihrer melodischen Beschaffenheit lexikalisch zu ordnen." *Sammelbände der internationalen Musikgesellschaft* 4:1–15.

Krohn, Ilmari. 1902–3. "Welche ist die beste Methode, um volks- und volksmässige Lieder nach ihrer melodischen (nicht textlichen) Beschaffenheit lexikalisch zu ordnen?" *Sammelbände der internationalen Musikgesellschaft* 4:643–60.

———.1907. "Über das lexikalische Ordnen von Volksmelodien." *Bericht über den zweiten Kongress der Internationalen Musikgesellschaft zu Basel,* 66–74.

Kuckertz, Josef. 1963. *Gestaltvariation in den von Bartók gesammelten rumänischen Colinden.* Regensburg: Gustav Bosse.

Lane, Edward William. 1966. *Manners and Customs of the Modern Egyptians.* London: J.M. Dent. First published 1836.

Larson, LeRoy. 1974. *Scandinavian-American Folk Dance Music.* Vol. 1: *The Norwegians in Minnesota.* Minneapolis: Banjar (BR-1825).

Leary, James P. 1982. "Polish Priests and Tavern Keepers in Portage County, Wisconsin." *Midwestern Journal of Language and Folklore* 8 (1): 34–42.

————.1984. "Old Time Music in Northern Wisconsin." *American Music* 2 (1): 71–87.

————.1986a. *Accordions in the Cutover: Field Recordings of Ethnic Music from Lake Superior's South Shore.* 2 discs. Ashland, Wis.: Northland College.

————.1986b. *Accordions in the Cutover: Field Recordings of Ethnic Music from Lake Superior's South Shore.* Descriptive booklet, with transcriptions and musical analysis by Philip V. Bohlman. Ashland, Wis.: Northland College.

Lerdahl, Fred, and Ray Jackendoff. 1983. *A Generative Theory of Tonal Music.* Cambridge, Mass: MIT Press.

Lévi-Strauss, Claude. 1966. *The Savage Mind.* Chicago: University of Chicago Press.

Levy, Marion J., Jr. 1966. *Modernization and the Structure of Societies: A Setting for International Affairs.* 2 vols. Princeton, N.J.: Princeton University Press.

Levy, Paul. 1911. *Geschichte des Begriffes Volkslied.* Berlin: Mayer und Müller.

List, George. 1978. "The Distribution of a Melodic Formula: Diffusion or Polygenesis." *Yearbook of the International Folk Music Council* 10:33–52.

————.1985. "Hopi Melodic Concepts." *Journal of the American Musicological Society* 38 (1):143–52.

Lloyd, A.L. 1967. *Folk Song in England.* London: Lawrence and Wishart.

Lockwood, Yvonne. 1984. "East Europeans: Local, Regional, and Ethnic Identity." *Journal of Folklore Research* 21 (2–3):221–22.

Loeb, Laurence D. 1972. "The Jewish Musician and the Music of Fars." *Asian Music* 4 (1):3–14.

Lomax, Alan. 1960. *The Folk Songs of North America in the English Language.* Garden City, N.Y.: Doubleday.

————.1968. *Folk Song Style and Culture.* Washington, D.C.: American Association for the Advancement of Science.

————.1976. *Cantometrics.* Berkeley: University of California Extension.

Long, Eleanor R. 1973. "Ballad Singers, Ballad Makers, and Ballad Etiology." *Western Folklore* 32 (4):225–36.

Lord, Albert B. 1960. *The Singer of Tales.* Cambridge, Mass : Harvard University Press.

Lortat-Jacob, Bernard. 1981. "Community Music as an Obstacle to Professionalism: A Berber Example." *Ethnomusicology* 25 (1):87–98.

————.1984. "Music and Complex Societies: Control and Management of Musical Production." *Yearbook for Traditional Music* 16:19–33.

Lu Zhiwei (C.W. Luh). 1984. "Folk Songs Ancient and Modern." In Lu Shuxiang, ed., *Five Lectures on Chinese Poetry.* Hong Kong: Joint Publishing Co.

Lysloff, René T.A., and Jim Matson. 1985. "A New Approach to the Classification of Sound-Producing Instruments." *Ethnomusicology* 29 (2):213–36.

McCulloh, Judith. 1970. " 'In the Pines': The Melodic-Textual Identity of an American Lyric Folksong Cluster." Ph.D. dissertation, Indiana University.

————.1983. "The Problem of Identity in Lyric Folk Song." In James Porter, ed., *The Ballad Image: Essays Presented to Bertrand Harris Bronson.* Los Angeles: Center for the Study of Comparative Folklore and Mythology, University of California, Los Angeles.

McMillan, Douglas J. 1964. "A Survey of Theories Concerning the Oral Transmission of the Traditional Ballad." *Southern Folklore Quarterly* 28 (4):299–309.

Malone, Bill C. 1979. *Southern Music/American Music.* Lexington: The University Press of Kentucky.

Martin, Philip, et al. 1986. *Ach Ya! Traditional German-American Music from Wisconsin.* 2 discs. Dodgeville: Wisconsin Folklife Center.

Massoudieh, Mohammad T. 1978. *Radif vocal de la musique traditionelle de l'Iran.* Teheran: Ministry of Culture and Fine Arts.

Merriam, Alan P. 1964. *The Anthropology of Music.* Evanston, Ill.: Northwestern University Press.

————.1967. *Ethnomusicology of the Flathead Indians.* Chicago: Aldine.

————.1979. "Basongye Musicians and Institutionalized Social Deviance." *Yearbook for Traditional Music* 11:1–26.

————.1982. "The Bala Musician." In idem, *African Music in Perspective.* Westport, Conn.: Greenwood Press.

Minnesota Scandinavian Ensemble. 1976. *Scandinavian-American Folk Dance Music.* Vol. 2: *Wisconsin Fiddle Music, Other Old Time.* Minneapolis: Banjar (BR-1828).

Mosely, Patricia. 1964. "Criteria for the Melodic Classification of Folksongs." *North Carolina Folklore* 12 (2):9–13.

Naumann, Hans. 1922. *Grundzüge der deutschen Volkskunde.* Leipzig: Quelle und Meyer.

Nettl, Bruno. 1956. *Music in Primitive Culture.* Cambridge, Mass.: Harvard University Press.

————.1957. "The Hymns of the Amish: An Example of Marginal Survival." *Journal of American Folklore* 70:323–38.

————.1973. *Folk and Traditional Music of the Western Continents.* 2d ed. Englewood Cliffs, N.J.: Prentice-Hall.

————.1976. *Folk Music in the United States: An Introduction.* 3d ed., rev. and expanded by Helen Myers. Detroit: Wayne State University Press.

————.1978. "Some Aspects of the History of World Music in the Twentieth Century: Questions, Problems, and Concepts," *Ethnomusicology* 22 (1):123–36.

————.1982. "Types of Tradition and Transmission." In Robert Falck and Timothy Rice, eds., *Cross-Cultural Perspectives on Music.* Toronto: University of Toronto Press.

————.1983. *The Study of Ethnomusicology: Twenty-nine Issues and Concepts.* Urbana: University of Illinois Press.

————.1985. *The Western Impact on World Music: Change, Adaptation, and Survival.* New York: Schirmer.

Nettl, Bruno, and Bela Foltin, Jr. 1972. *Daramad of Chahargah: A Study in the Performance Practice of Persian Music.* Detroit: Information Coordinators.

Neuman, Daniel M. 1976. "Towards an Ethnomusicology of Culture Change in Asia." *Asian Music* 7 (2):1–5.

Nketia, J.H. Kwabena. 1963. *Folk Songs of Ghana.* Legon: University of Ghana Press.

————.1974. *The Music of Africa.* New York: Norton.

Olsen, Dale A. 1980. "Symbol and Function in South American Indian Music." In Elizabeth May, ed., *Musics of Many Cultures: An Introduction.* Berkeley: University of California Press.

Ong, Walter J. 1982. *Orality and Literacy: The Technologizing of the Word.* London: Methuen.

Parry, C. Hubert H. 1910. *The Evolution of the Art of Music.* New York: Appleton.

Paulin, Don. 1980. *Das Folk-Music-Lexikon.* Frankfurt am Main: Fischer.

Peacock, James L. 1968. *Rites of Modernization: Symbolic and Social Aspects of Indonesian Proletarian Drama.* Chicago: University of Chicago Press.

Poladian, Sirvart. 1942. "The Problem of Melodic Variation in Folk Song." *Journal of American Folklore* 55:204–11.

Porter, James. 1976. "Jeannie Robertson's *My Son David:* A Conceptual Performance Model." *Journal of American Folklore* 89:7–26.

————.1978. "Introduction: The Traditional Music of Europeans in America." *Selected Reports in Ethnomusicology* 3 (1):1–23.

————.1985 "Parody and Satire as Mediators of Change in the Traditional Songs of Belle Stewart." In Carol L. Edwards and Kathleen E.B. Manley, eds., *Narrative Folksong: New Directions. Essays in Appreciation of W. Edson Richmond.* Boulder, Colo.: Westview Press.

————.1986. "Ballad Explanations, Ballad Reality, and the Singer's Epistemics," *Western Folklore* 45:110–25.

Porterfield, Nolan. 1979. *Jimmie Rodgers: The Life and Times of America's Blue Yodeler.* Urbana: University of Illinois Press.

Powers, Harold. 1970. "An Historical and Comparative Approach to the Classification of Ragas (with an Appendix on Ancient Indian Tunings)." *Selected Reports* 1 (3):1–78.

Pulikowski, Julian von. 1933. *Geschichte des Begriffes Volkslied im musikalischen Schrifttum: Ein Stück deutscher Geistesgeschichte.* Heidelberg: Carl Winters.

Racy, Ali Jihad. 1985. "Music and Dance in Lebanese Proverbs," *Asian Music* 17 (1):83–97.

Randolph, Vance, ed. 1980. *Ozark Folksongs.* 4 vols. Columbia: University of Missouri Press.

Redfield, Robert, and Milton Singer. 1962. "The Cultural Role of Cities." In Margaret Park Redfield, ed., *Human Nature and the Study of Society: The Papers of Robert Redfield.* Chicago: University of Chicago Press.

Reinhard, Kurt. 1975. "Bemerkungen zu den Âşik, den Volkssängern der Türkei." *Asian Music* 6 (1 and 2):189–206.

Reyes Schramm, Adelaida. 1982. "Explorations in Urban Ethnomusicology: Hard Lessons from the Spectacularly Ordinary," *Yearbook for Traditional Music* 14:1–14.

Ricoeur, Paul. 1971. "The Model of the Text: Meaningful Action Considered as Text." *Social Research* 38:529–62.

Robeson, Paul. 1958. *Here I Stand.* London: Dennis Dobson.

Rosen, Lawrence. 1984. *Bargaining for Reality: The Construction of Social Relations in a Muslim Community.* Chicago: University of Chicago Press.

Rosenberg, Neil V. 1985. *Bluegrass: A History.* Urbana: University of Illinois Press.

Roth, Klaus, and Juliana Roth. 1985. "A Bulgarian Professional Street Singer and His Songs." In Carol L. Edwards and Kathleen E.B. Manley, eds., *Narrative Folksong: New Directions. Essays in Appreciation of W. Edson Richmond.* Boulder, Colo.: Westview Press.

Royce, Anya Peterson. 1982. *Ethnic Identity: Strategies for Diversity.* Bloomington: Indiana University Press.

Sachs, Curt. 1929. *Geist und Werden der Musikinstrumente.* Berlin: J. Bard.

———.1940. *The History of Musical Instruments.* New York: Norton.

———.1962. *The Wellsprings of Music.* Ed. by Jaap Kunst. The Hague: Martinus Nijhoff.

Sadie, Stanley, ed. 1980. *The New Grove Dictionary of Music and Musicians.* London: Macmillan.

Sakata, Hiromi Lorraine. 1983. *Music in the Mind: The Concept of Music and Musician in Afghanistan.* Kent, Ohio: Kent State University Press.

Salmen, Walter. 1954. "Erk, Ludwig Christian." In Friedrich Blume, ed., *Die Musik in Geschichte und Gegenwart.* Vol. 3, columns 1496–1500. Kassel: Bärenreiter.

Sambamoorthy, P. 1952, *A Dictionary of South Indian Music and Musicians.* Vol. 1. Madras: Indian Music Publishing House.

de Saussure, Ferdinand. 1966. *Course in General Linguistics.* New York: McGraw-Hill.

Saygun, Ahmed Adnan. 1951. "Authenticity in Folk Music." *Journal of the International Folk Music Council* 3:7–10.

Schaeffner, André. 1936. *Origine des instruments de musique.* Paris: Payot.

Schmidt, Leopold. 1970. *Volksgesang und Volkslied: Proben und Probleme.* Berlin: Erich Schmidt.

Schneider, Albrecht. 1976. *Musikwissenschaft und Kulturkreislehre: Zur Methodik und Geschichte der Vergleichenden Musikwissenschaft.* Bonn-Bad Godesberg: Verlag für systematische Musikwissenschaft.

Schuyler, Philip D. 1979. "Rwais and Aḥwash: Opposing Tendencies in Moroccan Berber Music." *The World of Music* 1979 (1):65–80.

———.1984 "Berber Professional Musicians in Performance." In Gerard Béhague, ed.,

Performance Practice: Ethnomusicological Perspectives. Westport, Conn.: Greenwood Press.

Schwab, Heinrich W. 1973. "Das Vereinslied des 19. Jahrhunderts," In Rolf Wilhelm Brednich, Lutz Röhrich, and Wolfgang Suppan, eds., Die *Gattungen des Volkliedes.* Vol. 1. Munich: Wilhelm Fink.

————.1982. *Die Anfänge des weltlichen Berufsmusikertums in der mittelalterlichen Stadt: Studie zu einer Berufs- und Sozialgeschichte des Stadtmusikantentums.* Kassel: Bärenreiter.

Scott, John Anthony. 1983. *The Ballad of America: The History of the United States in Song and Story.* Carbondale: Southern Illinois University Press.

Sebeok, Thomas A. 1979. *The Sign and Its Masters.* Austin: University of Texas Press.

Seeger, Charles. 1949–50. "Oral Tradition in Music." In Maria Leach, ed., *Funk and Wagnalls Standard Dictionary of Folklore, Mythology, and Legend.* New York: Funk and Wagnalls.

————.1966. "Versions and Variants of 'Barbara Allen' in the Archive of American Folk Song in the Library of Congress." *Selected Reports* 1 (1):120–67

————.1977. "Professionalism and Amateurism in the Study of Folk Music." In idem, *Studies in Musicology 1935–1974.* Berkeley: University of California Press.

Sharp, Cecil J. 1965. *English Folk Song: Some Conclusions.* 4th ed., rev. by Maud Karpeles. Belmont, Cal.: Wadsworth. First edition 1907.

Shepard, Leslie. 1962. *The Broadside Ballad: A Study in Origins and Meaning.* London: Herbert Jenkins.

Shiloah, Amnon. 1974 "Le poète-musicien et la création poético-musicale au Moyen-Orient." *Yearbook of the International Folk Music Council* 6:52–63.

Shiloah, Amnon, and Erik Cohen. 1983. "The Dynamics of Change in Jewish Oriental Ethnic Music." *Ethnomusicology* 1983 (2):227–52.

Slobin, Mark. 1976. *Music in the Culture of Northern Afghanistan.* Tucson: University of Arizona Press.

Slyomovics, Susan. In press. *The Merchant of Art: An Egyptian Hilali Epic Poet in Performance.* Berkeley: University of California Press.

Smith, Barbara Herrenstein. 1984. "Contingencies of Values," In Robert von Hallberg, ed., *Canons.* Chicago: University of Chicago Press.

Sorce Keller, Marcello. 1984. "The Problem of Classification in Folksong Research: A Short History." *Folklore* 95 (1):100–104.

Spitzer, John, and Neal Zaslaw. 1986. "Improvised Ornamentation in Eighteenth-Century Orchestras." *Journal of the American Musicological Society* 39 (3):524–77.

Spottswood, Richard. 1982. "Ethnic and Popular Style in America." In William Ferris and Mary L. Hunt, eds., *Folk Music and Modern Sound.* Jackson: University Press of Mississippi.

Stafford, William C. 1830. *A History of Music.* Edinburgh: Constable.

Stern, Stephen. 1977. "Ethnic Folklore and the Folklore of Ethnicity." *Western Folklore* 36 (1):7–32.

Stumpf, Carl. 1911. *Die Anfänge der Musik.* Leipzig: J.A. Barth.

Suppan, Wolfgang. 1973(?). "Zur Verwendung der Begriffe Gestalt, Struktur, Modell und Typus in der Musikethnologie." In Doris Stockmann and Jan Stęszewski, eds., *Analyse und Klassifikation von Volksmelodien.* Kraków: Polskie Wydawnictwo Muzyczne.

Szwed, John F. 1970. "Paul E. Hall: A Newfoundland Song-Maker and His Community of Song." In Henry Glassie et al., eds., *Folksongs and Their Makers.* Bowling Green, Ohio: Bowling Green University Popular Press.

Tappert, Wilhelm. 1890. *Wandernde Melodien.* 2d ed., enlarged. Leipzig: List und Francke.

Temo. 1981. *Temo, barde du Kurdistan: La tradition et l'exil.* Paris: Ocora.

Thorp, N. Howard. 1966. *Songs of the Cowboys.* Ed. by Austin E. and Alta S. Fife. New York: Potter.

Trevor-Roper, Hugh. 1983. "The Invention of Tradition: The Highland Tradition of Scotland." In Eric Hobsbawm and Terence Ranger, eds., *The Invention of Tradition.* Cambridge: Cambridge University Press.

Turner, Victor. 1969. *The Ritual Process: Structure and Anti-Structure.* Chicago: Aldine.

Väisänen, A.O. 1949. "Suggestions for the Methodical Classification and Investigation of Folk Tunes." *Journal of the International Folk Music Council* 1:34–35.

Vansina, Jan. 1985. *Oral Tradition as History.* Madison: University of Wisconsin Press.

Vaughan Williams, Ralph. 1954. *National Music.* New York: Oxford University Press.

Wallaschek, Richard. 1893. *Primitive Music: An Inquiry into the Origin and Development of Music, Song, Instruments, Dances and Pantomimes of Savage Races.* London: Longmans, Green.

Wallis, Roger, and Krister Malm. 1984. *Big Sounds for Small Peoples: The Music Industry in Small Countries.* New York: Pendragon.

Warkov, Esther. 1986. "Revitalization of Iraqi Jewish Instrumental Traditions in Israel: The Persistent Centrality of an Outsider Tradition." *Asian Music* 17 (2):9–31.

Ward, John M. 1986. "The Morris Tune." *Journal of the American Musicological Society* 39 (3):294–331.

Waterman, Richard A. 1952. "African Influence on the Music of the Americas." In Sol Tax, ed., *Acculturation in the Americas.* Chicago: University of Chicago Press.

Whisnant, David E. 1983. *All That Is Native and Fine: The Politics of Culture in an American Region.* Chapel Hill: University of North Carolina Press.

Wilgus, D.K. 1971. "Country-Western Music and the Urban Hillbilly," In Américo Paredes and Ellen J. Stekert, eds., *The Urban Experience and Folk Tradition.* Austin: University of Texas Press.

Will, G.F. 1909. "Songs of Western Cowboys." *Journal of American Folk-Lore* 22:258–59.

Wiora, Walter. 1949. "Concerning the Conception of Authentic in Folk Music." *Journal of the International Folk Music Council* 1:14–19.

———.1953. *Europäischer Volksgesang.* Cologne: Arno Volk.

———.1957. *Europäische Volksmusik und abendländische Tonkunst.* Kassel: Bärenreiter.

———.1965. *The Four Ages of Music.* Trans. by M.D. Herder Norton. New York: Norton.

———.1971a "Reflections on the Problem: How Old Is the Concept Folksong?" *Yearbook of the International Folk Music Council* 3:23–33.

———.1971b *Das deutsche Lied: Zur Geschichte und Ästhetik einer musikalischen Gattung.* Wolfenbüttel: Möseler.

Wong, Isabel K.F. 1984. "*Geming Gequ:* Songs for the Education of the Masses." In Bonnie S. McDougall, ed., *Popular Chinese Literature and Performing Arts in the People's Republic of China, 1949–1979.* Berkeley: University of California Press.

Wright, Rochelle, and Robert L. Wright. 1983. *Danish Emigrant Ballads and Songs.* Carbondale: Southern Illinois University Press.

Yung, Bell. 1984. "Choreographic and Kinesthetic Elements in Performance on the Chinese Seven-String Zither." *Ethnomusicology* 28 (3):505–17.

INDEX

Abrahams, Roger D., 22
Accordions in folk music, 116
Acquired musical roles, 81–82
Additions to folk music, 23–24
Adhān, defined, 99
Aerophones, defined, 37. *See also* Musical instruments in folk music
Afghani folk music, 41–42, 90, 91, 98
Afghani folk musicians, 101
African folk music, 71, 81. *See also specific types of African folk music*
Agelessness of folk music. *See* Timelessness of folk music
Aḥādīth, defined, 97
Aḥwash, defined, 100. *See also* Berber folk music
Allgemeine Lieder, defined, 114
Ambitus, 38, 41, 47
Amish folk music, 18, 59
Anderson, Benedict, 108–109, 111
Anthologies of folk music, 65. *See also specific anthologies of folk music*
"Anyuan Lukuang gongren julebu buge" (Shaoqi), 107, 108
Apollo, 4
Appalachian folk music, 45, 50
Arabic folk music. *See* Middle Eastern folk music
Arnim, Achim von, 7
Art music: characteristics of, 47–49, 139; and folk music, 46–50, 90, 129, 134, 139. *See also* Classical music, defined
Ascribed musical roles, 81–82
ᶜ*Asheq*, 59, 92–93, 101. *See also* Islam, music in; Middle Eastern folk music
Assimilation of folk music, 20. *See also* Consolidation of folk music
Attali, Jacques, 56, 95
Audiences of folk music, 73–74
Authenticity of folk music, 17, 130–31; changes in folk music compared to, 10, 11; characteristics of, 10, 13, 130; defined, 10

Balkan folk music, 83
Ballads, 16, 38, 71. *See also specific types of ballads*
Banjos in folk music, 115
Bänkelsänger, 84
Bannen, Charles, 59–60, 75
"Barbara Allen" (folk song), 75, 76

Barry, Phillips, folk music research of, 8, 24, 27, 28, 69
Bartók, Béla, 54; classification of folk music by, 40–41, 45, 46, 49, 50; as composer, 47, 48–49; folk music research of, 47, 101–102
Basongye folk music, 83, 86
Bauer, Michael, 133
Baul folk music, 83
Bayard, Samuel P., 23–24
Beethoven, Ludwig van, 48
Benjamin, Walter, 121
Berber folk music, 93, 100
Blacking, John, 4
Blind persons, as folk musicians, 83
Bluegrass, 129–30, 133
Blues, 38
Blum, Stephen, 44–45, 92
Bohemian-American folk music, 116
Bohlman, Philip, xii
Borges, Jorge Luis, 121
Borrowing of folk music, 20–21, 28. *See also* Consolidation of folk music
Brentano, Clemens, 7
Bricolage, 116–17
Bridges in folk music, 27
Broadside ballads, 21, 28–29, 65, 84–85. *See also* Ballads
Bronson, Bertrand H., 39
Broonzy, Big Bill, 87, 88

Campbell, Olive Dame, 45
Canadian folk music, 73
Canons of folk music, xviii, 39, 50–51; in Chinese folk music, 107; defined, 104; formation of, 105–19, 128; functions of, 104, 105; in German folk music, 113; imagined, 111–12, 116–19; in Israeli folk music, 117, 119; mediated, 111, 112, 114–16; and modernization, 107–109, 112; and nationalism, 117; in oral tradition of folk music, 30–32; small-group, 111, 112–14; in Southern folk music, 109
Cante-fable, 7
Cantometrics, 42, 43, 56. *See also* Lomax, Alan
Changes in folk music: authenticity of folk music compared to, 10, 11; characteristics of, 10–11, 13, 26, 27–28, 73, 76, 92, 128, 134; defined, 10; and folk musicians, xix, 73, 84, 86, 102; and modernization, 132, 139; in oral tradition of folk music, 18–24, 25, 26–27, 28, 30, 31–32; responses to, 132–35; types of, 10–